PROPERTY INVESTMENT SECRETS

RENT

TO

RENT

A COMPLETE RENTAL PROPERTY INVESTING GUIDE

SAM WELLMAN

First Printed in Great Britain by
Obex Publishing Ltd in 2019

2 4 6 8 10 9 7 5 3 1

ISBN 978 1 913454 00 5

A CIP catalogue record for this book is available
from the British Library

Obex Publishing Limited
Reg. No. 12169917

CONTENTS

INTRODUCTION.. 7

CHAPTER 1: ORIENTATION TO SUBLETTING..........19

DEFINING RENT-TO-RENT AND ITS MAIN CHARACTERS. 21

HOW IT WORKS..23

RISKS OF SUBLETTING..26

BENEFITS OF SUBLETTING...29

THREE BASIC SUBLET MODELS 32

PERSONAL PREPARATION 44

CHAPTER 2: SETTING A BUSINESS FOUNDATION ..56

THE ETHICAL MIDDLEMAN..58

WHAT NOT TO DO..65

DETERMINING YOUR MOST VIABLE RENTAL MODEL......73

YOUR 12-MONTH BUSINESS PLAN AND ANNUAL GROWTH

GOALS...82

CHAPTER 3: THE BUSINESS SETUP 92

SELECT A BUSINESS STRUCTURE.......................................94

JOIN THE PRS 101

GATHER YOUR CONTRACTS..104

GDPR COMPLIANCE...106

SET UP YOUR PROFESSIONAL IMAGE AND STATUS 115

CHAPTER 4: 5-STEP PROCESS TO FIND RENTAL

PROPERTIES 126

STEP 1: LOCATION, LOCATION, LOCATION 128

STEP 2: FIND VIABLE PROPERTIES 131

STEP 3: INVESTIGATE RELEVANT LOCAL CODES AND

REGULATIONS 133

STEP 4: SIZE UP LOCAL COMPETITION 134

STEP 5: RUN THE NUMBERS 135

CHAPTER 5: YOUR VIEWING AND SIGNING

PROCESS **136**

VIEWING & NEGOTIATIONS WITH PROPERTY OWNERS 138

THE CONTRACT AND THE CLOSE 145

VIEWING AND NEGOTIATIONS WITH TENANTS 152

FINDING TENANTS AND CONDUCTING VIEWINGS 161

PRE-SCREENING QUESTIONS TO ASK PROSPECTIVE

TENANTS 162

CHAPTER 6: SCALING FOR SUCCESS 167

ACQUIRE A TEAM 170

GROW THE MARKETING GAME....................................... 172

GET INVOLVED THE COMMUNITY 178

ADVANCE YOURSELF 180

CONCLUSION 185

Introduction

Congratulations on your purchase of Property Investment Secrets - Rent to Rent: A Complete Property Investing Guide. You've just made the first move in establishing a rent-to-rent business that will pay off for a long while to come. Purchasing this book is the first step to success - it shows you are willing to learn and ready to take action. You may have already read my second book "Property Investment Secrets – Rent to Rent: You've Got Questions, I've Got Answers!" however this book is laid out as a step by step walkthrough guide, which follows the KISS principle that keeps things straightforward to understand. After reading this guide, you may have some burning questions or just need more information. If that's the case I recommend you check out my second Rent-to-Rent book which addresses everything you could possibly need to know!

Most people already know that buy to let investing strategy can yield great returns, and therefore they appreciate the fundamentals behind the buy to let business model.

The rent-to-rent model has become increasingly more popular in the last few years, mainly because you can get started with little to no investment. In most cases, the most you can expect to invest is one month's rent upfront and the cost of renovation. As your negotiation skills improve, you will see that it is very easy to get landlords to agree to no deposits in return for a long term guaranteed rental agreement.

With regards to renovation, we are not talking about finding a run-down property that needs a new kitchen and bathroom and possibly damp proofing. What you need to remember is you will not own the property, ever. It is in your best interest to find somewhere with minimal work to do. However, if you want to use one of the strategies discussed in this book, there are several requirements and changes that you may need to make to the property. I will cover all of this later, don't worry.

In 2014, I paid £1,500 for a two-day property course in London. I had no money at the time, so this type of investment would seem ridiculous to most people, so I kept it quiet. I had been spending most of my time researching ways to make a passive income, and property investing always seemed to top every list I came across, so I decided to take action.

I felt that 90% of the course was filled with completely useless information to me at the time because I had no money to invest. I made lots of notes throughout, knowing that one day they should be beneficial. In the afternoon during the 2nd day of the course, after I had started to question why I had spent such a large sum of money on this training, the rent-to-rent strategy was discussed. It changed my life as I then realised that £1,500 was soon becoming the best investment I have ever made. Throughout this book I will be providing you with everything I learned that day about the rent-to-rent model, and everything else I have learned since!

As you're about to learn, rent-to-rent can be a quick way to grow money, but it's by no means a "set-it-and-forget-it" business. Rent-to-rent will take your time and effort to understand and implement legitimately. Still, if you digest the lessons and expertise in this book, you'll be able to act fast and grow strong within your first 12 months. When executed correctly, you can expect between £400-£1200 monthly income for each property, and this shows that it is not too difficult to replace your job with your rent-to-rent income.

Inside this book, you'll find what is essentially my crash course on building a rent-to-rent business. You'll learn my secrets and mistakes so that your growth will be even more successful than mine. You will become familiar with the definition of rent-to-rent and what it takes for you to succeed. You will have an appreciation of the risks and

benefits associated with the business and how to
select the right sublet model and business structure
to get you off the ground with little to no start-up
capital. I'll teach you what you need to know, and
what you need to do to be an ethical rent-to-rent
professional, instead of an untrustworthy charmer
with a quickly dissolving business.

This book aims to give you everything you need,
from contracts to regulations and codes, so that you
can run a respectable business that cultivates
excellence and supporting the communities you rent
to. You'll find there are a good number of
individuals that come into this business with no
intention of following the rules and representing the
profession with honour. If this is your plan, this
book is not for you. But if you want to be a well-
founded and lawful authority in the world of rent-
to-rent and beyond, you're education starts here.

By the time you have completed this book, you
should have learned the essentials of creating an
ethical rent-to-rent business, with a well-thought-
out business plan. You will have selected a business
structure that suits you and understood the
importance of following GDPR compliance in your
business. The simple 5-step process to find the
perfect location and the perfect properties to manage
will be essential to you. In addition, there is
guidance on how to negotiate with property owners;

how to complete a successful showing of the property you manage; how to pre-screen tenants and how to secure the final contract. Upon completion, you will know exactly what must happen next to take your business to the next level and develop an ongoing route to achieve maximum success in the rent-to-rent arena.

"What is rent-to-rent?"

Whether you've had experience in real estate or you're brand new to it, you may have heard the term "rent to own" or "rent to buy" in which a tenant rents out a property as their residence, with the intention to buy it from the property owner. The term "rent to rent" is a supplement to that, and it's exactly what it sounds like. An individual rents out a property from a landlord, with the intent to then rent it back out to others. In this case, the individual (the renter) most often does not live at that residence, and it's intended that a third-party (the subletter) will reside in the property instead.

Rent-to-rent is sometimes referred to as "guaranteed rent" because, in the vast majority of these agreements, the renter agrees to pay the property owner a guaranteed and fixed cost each month regardless of whether the subletter has paid all, some, or none of the monthly rent. In fact, even during periods where no subletter resides at the property, like the period of time in-between subletters moving in and out, the renter still pays the property owner a guaranteed rent. This is one of the major benefits that tempts a property owner to such an agreement.

In addition to guaranteed rent, most sublet agreements state that the renter also assumes property management and all of the work and cost that comes with it. These are the two main benefits that make a rent-to-rent offer so appealing to property owners.

"Isn't Subletting illegal?"

Depending on who you ask, you may have heard
that subletting is legal, or you may have heard the
opposite. In truth, subletting a property is 100%
legal- so long as you follow the rules. There are two
cardinal rules that ensure your rent-to-rent
operation is legitimate.

First, you must have permission from the property
owner to conduct a sublet scenario within the
property. Some less legitimate people think if the
landlord didn't specifically say no subletting is
allowed, then it's allowed. Not true. You must have
written consent from the property owner, within
your contract, to manage a sublet legally. You've
heard the expression, "It's easier to ask for
forgiveness than permission", but in this case that
statement is most definitely incorrect. Asking for
forgiveness after conducting an illegal sublet is much
more damaging to both you and the property owner
(and the subletter) and consequently, the legal
implications are much greater.

In some cases, the property owner may not own the
property outright, but rather, pays a mortgage on
the property. Some lenders state specifically that a
mortgaged property is not allowed to engage in
subletting, as it puts a considerably higher amount
of stress and wear-and-tear on a property when

there's frequent resident turnover. In other cases, the insurance company that covers the property may have a similar stipulation against subletting. In both cases, if these terms are compromised, the property owner risks losing the property insurance or the property mortgage (or both). This doesn't end up being just the property owner's problem; it's yours too, as you are the organiser of the sublet.

The second cardinal rule is that your contracts must be bona fide contracts. When you come to an agreement with the property owner, this contract should not be the standard type of rental agreement, but rather, should make clear and specific terms and conditions concerning the sublet operation. As you move through these chapters, you'll see that there are several other rules you need to follow when it comes to running a legal rent-to-rent business, but these two are the most crucial, and really, the foundations to the sublet operation as a whole.

"Is this book right for me?"

This book is for you if...

You've ever been curious about what it takes to start a rent-to-rent business. At some point in your experience, you may have heard that subletting rental properties was a great way to make money quickly. Perhaps you want to explore exactly what's involved in starting that venture, but you'd rather find out from someone who's done it than find out first hand and risk significant failure. You're probably smarter than the average Joe, and you know it can't be so easy. No business worth developing is ever a piece of cake. You're right, and if you keep reading, you'll find that is exactly the case in each of these sections.

You're a brand new rent-to-rent business, but you're not quite sure if you're established properly, following the rules, or setting the strategies that will help you to succeed. If you find yourself in this predicament, you are certainly not alone. If you don't know exactly where you are in the process, or worse still is when you don't have a process, the techniques and instructions in this book can help you identify where you are and where you'd like to be. These lessons will give you the steps to get from here to there.

You're already an established rent-to-rent business but the process isn't moving as quickly as you'd like. It's possible that some of your processes need an overhaul or refinement. It could be that you're aiming too high and are over-ambitious. It could be because you lack the confidence to make the important business decisions. This book will stop the self-doubt and give you the confidence you need to take the next steps to collect your next rental payment.

You've been established a year or more but need to sharpen your aim and update your game. It's easy to get so busy that you forget to grow and develop yourself and seek out new opportunities that will advance your business. Use the information in this book to hone your skills and pull in new prospects and profits from places you forgot to look.

Or maybe you've read my other book "Property Investment Secrets – Rent to Rent: You've Got Questions, I've Got Answers!" and loved it, but wanted a step by step guide!

"How should I use this book for my business?"

With this book, it is my intention to walk you through the simple and the complex of creating a rent-to-rent business. The book is structured to give you an overview of general ideas and then dive more deeply into these ideas as you move through each section. The sections contain facts, experiences, and instructions to help you understand why each part of the overall process is so important and so crucial to making money. You will benefit most if you read this book cover to cover and then return to it often for reminders, techniques and guidance. This book is meant to be used as a field guide and on-going source of reference. Use this as you would use a text from any classroom. Cheat from it, steal from it, and make these techniques your own. Learn from it and come back to leave notes in the margin about how you've improved upon what I've taught you.

Chapter 1:

Orientation to Subletting

You've essentially found yourself at the start of a crash course on making money with subletting. If you're here, there's a high probability that your number one priority is making a profit quickly, and with the least amount of effort and work. Most probably, the idea of investing very little of your own money in order to start turning a significant profit is very appealing.

The idea of generating a small portfolio of rentals from which to make monthly recurring revenue is tantalising. The dream of quitting your job and doing rentals full time seems suddenly so close. It is close; it can be yours. You can manage a small portfolio of rent-to-rent properties that make you a fine supplemental income or even replace the income you're earning now. But you cannot be messy and lazy about the management of it. Do not think that this is an effortless income. As you will see, it does require a fair amount of your time and energy if you are to be successful.

To begin, we'll define key aspects of subletting and identify three of the most popular models used in rent-to-rent business regularly. You'll become acquainted, if you're not already, with what it means to manage rent-to-rent contracts. From what it takes, to what it pays, and all the legalities, formalities, and nitty-gritty work in between. We'll look at the pros and cons of rent-to-rent operations, and strategies you can put in place to ensure you profit quickly and cleanly.

Rent-to-rent is usually not the end goal; it's not the last stop. Most often, it's the first step in generating enough profit to use for bigger and better investment opportunities. As with anything, there are both positive and negative aspects of managing rent-to-rent properties, and we'll examine both.

The information in this section is meant to focus your attention and give you a bird's eye perspective on the overall business of operating rent-to-rent properties. Throughout this crash course, I hope to illustrate to you the lay of the land, the boundaries, and a glimpse of the lands beyond subletting.

Defining Rent-to-Rent and its Main Characters

Let's start at the very beginning and give meaning to the term "rent-to-rent". When we talk about rent-to-rent opportunities, what's meant is subletting. Subletting is the practice of leasing a property from a landlord or property owner, and then renting that unit out to another party for a higher price.

To keep it simple, there are three major players in a sublet scenario:

The Property Owner - This is the person with exclusive rights and control over the property you rent; the lessor

The Renter - That's you, the person renting from the property owner; the lessee.

The Subletter - The third party that rents the property from you at a higher price; the actual occupants of the property.

Local Authorities - In my experience, it helps to consider the fourth party however, since their influence is so great: authorities. This includes both national and local enforcers of housing regulation. It generally also includes any type of business law and regulation you may need to legitimately start your business. It's critical to count local authorities as key players in your business because the impacts are always going to be there and rather than try to go around and avoid them, it ends up being smarter, safer, and faster, in the long run, to approach these head-on. Consider it just another step necessary to successful subletting.

How It Works

It starts with a sublet agreement between you and the property owner. The agreement says that it's permissible for you to sublet your rented space to a third party in your stead. You'd naturally be able to do so because the property would not be your own residence, or you'd often not be at the location for longer periods of time (think travel, school, etc).

Next, an agreement is made between you and the third party to rent the property at a higher cost than that which you pay to the property owner. This, of course, gives you the opportunity to make a profit on the management of the property. This is great for the subletter because they have a well-managed place to reside. It's great for the property owner because they receive a monthly income they can depend on. It's great for you, obviously, for the profit.

In most cases, however, managing the property instead of the owner, and subletting to another party in your place, comes with a handful of responsibility you need to be aware of and prepared for. More than likely, most landlords will be sceptical when you approach them with an offer. This means that you need to have a couple of attractive factors to get a deal that seems good for both parties.

Of course, this comes down to the art of negotiation, but I always tell landlords that all maintenance and general repairs will be upheld by myself. These include general decoration duties and any damage to small items. Structural issues and large repairs, such as window replacement or central heating, will be covered by the property owner. It is essential that this is crystal clear within your contracts.

Another sweetener is to offer the landlord a guaranteed rent for up to 5 years. Of course, I normally start with 2 years, and try to push for no more than a 3-year deal – however when I started, I was so keen to get a property deal I signed a 5-year agreement, but managed to reduce rental payments by £375 a month.

You may be asking yourself why would any landlord ever agree to this, and the answer is simple. As long as you cover the cost of their mortgage payments (if they have one) then they are a having their house paid for without any hassle, without any issues from tenants, without any periods with their house being vacant, and without any agency fees. In addition, in most cases, the property is also increasing in value often over and above the cost of inflation. These are just some of the reasons you can give to the landlord when they express their concerns, or preferably before they even get any doubt in their minds- in your original pitch.

Most importantly, if your subtenant fails to pay you rent on time, you're still responsible for ensuring the owner is paid on time.

Risks of Subletting

For a more comprehensive understanding of how rent-to-rent businesses work, next, we'll take a look at the risks and benefits that come with your new enterprise. Rent-to-rent is not for everyone, and it's critical you assess these factors before deciding to pursue business in this niche.

You're on the Line for Guaranteed Rent

While there are benefits to not owning the property, there are some very important risks to be aware of. Perhaps the most important, which I've mentioned briefly, is the obligation of ensuring your property owner is paid a guaranteed rent each month, regardless of whether your subletter pays (or pays on time). We'll take a look at this in greater detail in a later section and focus on the importance of screening your sublet prospects carefully and cautiously to ensure you're forming an agreement with a tenant that has a reliable history of paying rent on time. Taking accountability for this obligation is an important aspect of the agreement you make with your property owner. It's a big benefit to the owner and thus will act as a key point of leverage for you in coming to a sublet agreement.

Property Maintenance is on Your Tab

Another big benefit to the property owner, and thus another key piece of leverage in your sublet agreement, is relinquishing property management to you, both in terms of financial obligation and effort. In most cases, when you sublet, the upkeep and maintenance for the property is your cost. This is another crucial reason that screening subletters very well is very important.

You Pay Between Tenancy Gaps

For the property owner, this is a big benefit; for you, it's a risk you must plan for. When tenants move out, the property owner usually needs a month or more to handle cleaning and repairs before a new tenant can be signed for the accommodation. In the meantime, the property owner loses that monthly income. But with you subletting the property, the owner is guaranteed not to lose any monthly income between tenants. You'll be paying regardless. So this means you need to do a bit of work upfront to make sure you collect enough to pay rent to the owner during that eventuality. It also means you need to plan for a fast clean up and you need to get a new subletter into the space quickly. For this reason, rent-to-rent businesses should not wait until the month of the move-out to start making new plans. Have a tenant lined up and get cleaning and repairs done quickly (think: within a week).

No Capital Growth

Since you don't own anything in this scenario, it means you don't benefit from capital growth. Over time, the property will (usually) increase in value over time. Capital growth is a huge benefit to owning the property, but it doesn't mean anything to you. This is often why rent-to-rent businesses eventually use the profit they've generated through subletting to invest in a property they can own. This risk, however, does have a silver lining. If the property suffers a loss of value over time, you aren't affected.

Benefits of Subletting

You've Got the Upper Hand on Agents

A property owner seeking to rent out their property might initially turn to an agent for help acquiring legitimate tenants, but this isn't free for the owner and it doesn't address other ownership concerns like guaranteed rent and repair costs. Agents don't help with this, they simply market the property and screen prospective tenants. You, on the other hand, would typically agree to rental payment during gaps and property upkeep. This puts your offer ahead of the agent offer as it benefits the owner in bigger ways. For the owner, accepting a lower guaranteed rental cost from you in exchange for these benefits is often a much more cost-effective solution than paying an agent.

You Set the Rental Price

So you've found a property and an owner to work with you on subletting. If you're a good negotiator, you've been able to convince the owner to charge you a little less than what he or she would normally charge on the market. This can be a very attractive offer for the owner because, in exchange, you'll pay during gaps, manage the tenants, and take care of repairs and cleaning as needed. The benefit for you is that you pay a bit lower of a cost to the landlord each month and you can charge what you like, so long as it's in the range of market prices for the location. This offers you the opportunity to collect the most profit you can each month from the subletter after you've paid the owner your agreed-upon price.

No Stamp Duty or Property Conveyancing Costs

Another benefit of *not* being the property owner is that you're not responsible for Stamp Duty (SDLT), which is a required tax on land and property over £125,000 for residential, and over £150,000 for non-residential properties in England and Northern Ireland. In addition, you'll be able to skip the costly conveyancing process that typically requires a solicitor to finalise transfers and legalities of the property on your behalf. This closing and transfer process is thorough and therefore can take weeks or months to complete, but in a rent-to-rent situation, the finalising of agreements take much less effort and legal regulation and therefore can be wrapped up in several days.

No Mortgages to Secure and Pay

Perhaps the most significant benefit to you is the lack of mortgage work involved. Because you're renting from the property owner, it isn't necessary for you to secure mortgages, which cuts out a significant cost and risk. In many cases, individuals beginning a rent-to-rent business are doing so because they do not have the disposable capital to invest in a mortgage on a property, necessary property updates, and repairs. These same individuals often don't have the credit history necessary for a decent mortgage. In the case of a mortgage, not only are you up against capital and credit, you'll nearly always need a down payment of 20% and sometimes more. Rent-to-rent allows you to skip all this, and go more or less straight to the profit of the business. Accruing income this way allows for a fast and significant profit to be made, which can then be reinvested for more rent-to-rent properties, or perhaps used to establish the capital and credit history needed to branch into property ownership yourself.

Three Basic Sublet Models

As you can see from the benefits and risks of
subletting, you don't have as much overall control of
the property as the owner has. The owner could
essentially decide to forfeit the deal. The owner
might not pay the mortgage on the property
(assuming there is one) and the property could be
repossessed by the lender, leaving you out of pocket
and in a sticky spot for recuperating your business
loss. Owning a property does give you more control
over the entire situation. However, you've likely
turned to a rent-to-rent opportunity because you
don't have the necessary requirements to mortgage
and own the property. So how then, can you set
your business to profit as much as possible from a
rent-to-rent scenario? There are three basic models
for rent-to-rent business that sublet experts rely on
to make a generous profit that will help to grow and
scale the business. Let's take a look at each so you
can decide which model will work best for you.
Also, keep in mind that rent-to-rent businesses
building a portfolio may choose to sublet properties
under each of these models; you don't have to
choose just one. To start though, select the model
that will be easiest for you to secure and manage,
and then grow from there.

1: The Traditional AST Model

The AST model is the most common type of rental in the world of private rentals. AST means Assured Shorthold Tenancy and the lease is typically for 6 months or a year, and then it's subject to renewal. In this model, you rent a property from the owner and sublet the entire unit to one party. With this scenario, you'll negotiate with the owner to pay a lesser guaranteed monthly rent to make a profit from the subletter. This is probably the simplest model for rent-to-rent profit, but you'll need to sharpen those negotiation skills to ensure you're making a profit, especially after tenancy gaps, property management and repairs.

2: The HMO Model and HMO Regulations

An HMO property is a House of Multiple Occupancy. This means you'll have several subletters under one roof. This is not possible with a property suited for only one party, such as a one-bedroom apartment or flat. For each individual you sublet to, you must provide a bedroom; you cannot sublet more than one person to a bedroom. For this reason, if you're planning on subletting one unit to multiple parties, you'll need to find a property that contains multiple bedrooms and at least one receiving room, such as a living room. That said, if you find accommodation with, for example, three bedrooms which have always been rented to one family, you stand to make more profit by renting out each room to a separate tenant. At first glance, it may seem that an HMO unit may not be as desirable on the market but do carry out your due diligence. There are many situations in which prospective tenants find themselves benefitting from a shared living space like an HMO. If the unit is located near a university or an office and industrial neighbourhood, HMOs can do extremely well. Students and young, single, professionals are perfect prospects for an HMO. It goes without saying, that if you're planning on the HMO sublet model, you'll need to make sure your owner agrees to this as well, but if so, then you stand to make a greater profit. In many cases, one or two subletters can make up the guaranteed rent you'll owe the owner, but the additional tenants make up straight profit for your business.

This potential profit looks sensational, but be realistic. This type of model comes with some extra management you'll be responsible for.

First, you'll need to do a smart job in recruiting your tenants, and this means tenants that will get along amiably and not cause you undue personal stress. The good news is that when you sublet to an individual for an HMO, tenants typically expect to live with others they don't necessarily know and are ready to make general compromises with their flatmates to pay a smaller monthly rent themselves. Younger professionals and students are often already used to this type of living situation and make great tenants, so long as you seek out and sign the responsible ones with a decent rental history and stable financial background.

Second, an HMO rent-to-rent often comes with a slightly higher cost of management in terms of utility costs, repairs, and upkeep. Three or four parties in a space that used to house one party translates to a more aggressive use of the property and more wear-and-tear. More electricity, water and heat is used, and a greater bandwidth of internet access is needed, especially in the case of students and professionals.

Third, you need to make yourself aware of restrictions and regulations for an HMO property. For example, the property owner may be open to the idea of an HMO rental, but the mortgage lender may not be. Be sure to do your homework on what's legal and what, if any, licensing is needed for this type of operation. All of this considered, HMO properties are the most popular type of sublet model because of the additional profit than can be easily captured each month. If you're thorough in your search, you can find existing HMO properties that are currently underperforming and rectify this with updates, better management, and better tenants. This takes away a good deal of the upfront preparations and makes you a profit faster and with less effort. Marketing and screening are always going to be a major factor for you, so when you get to the stage of setting up your business and business model, consider these two factors and work them into your plan as a permanent requirement for yourself.

Fourth, if a property is not already set up to receive multiple occupancies, the cost is on you at the start to convert the unit according to relevant regulations.

There are many regulations and modifications

needed to operate an HMO, with unlimited fines for anyone running an HMO illegally. To start with, you will need to obtain an HMO Licence if you have 5 or more tenants in a property, forming two or more separate households, or the tenants share a kitchen, bathroom or toilet. For example, if you have a family of 4, plus a lodger, you will need to obtain a license. If you do not meet the above criteria, you may not need to obtain a license but all other regulations should be met to run your small HMO legally.

Different authorities have different requirements, so it is essential that you contact them to check, but I have included a list of common requirements.

All tenants need to sign an HMO tenancy agreement, and you should keep records of all of your tenant's details.

It is your responsibility to regularly check that all appliances are safe all year round, and repair anything as soon as you are made aware of any issues. Gas certificates will need to be sent into the local authorities annually, and electrical certification needs to be available upon request.

Smoke alarms need to be hard-wired in by an electrician on each floor, and you should also have carbon monoxide alarms fitted. You also need to make sure that all bedroom and kitchen doors are self-closing fire doors. Bedroom doors and external doors should have external key locks, with internal thumb turn locks, so in the case of a fire they can easily be unlocked for a quick evacuation. There should also be a fire notice board located in a communal area, such as the kitchen, with a clear evacuation plan for the tenants.

It is also good practice to include a cupboard and fridge/freezer organisation chart on the communal notice board. A good way to do this is to number every bedroom and then have parts of the fridge/freezer separated for each tenant, with a diagram indication which part belongs to each number. You can then put numbers on different cupboards and drawers in the kitchen, so every tenant has space for their food, drink and kitchen essentials.

Anyone under the age of 10 must have a room larger than or equal to 4.64 sqm. Anyone over the age of 10 must have a room larger than or equal to 6.51 sqm, and if a room is to be shared by two adults it must be larger than or equal to 10.22 sqm. The general rule is that there must be one bathroom for every four tenants. If you are looking at a four-bedroom property with the potential to convert a dining room into another bedroom, it must have at least two bathrooms.

You should also be obtaining a TV license on behalf

of the household, as it is good practice to provide a TV for the communal living room.

3: The Accommodation Model

Though traditionally this has been the least popular model to follow, its popularity is on the rise, especially with the development of Airbnb. The accommodation model can be your biggest profit maker if managed correctly. With this model, you rent a unit from the owner and then set the space for short-term accommodations, much like an Airbnb space or a hotel space. The space is then rented out to other parties for short periods of time, such as days or weeks; perhaps a month. In most cases, accommodation is rented out to holidaymakers and business professionals.

For a model like this to work successfully, there are a few points to keep in mind. First, you should make sure your owner is aware and happy to comply with this type of subletting. This type of arrangement means a much higher turnover of people coming in and out of the property, and this isn't necessarily something an owner would be happy with because of the general risk involved with the property. You might find that those staying in the accommodation don't respect the property and belongings as much as they would if they resided there. Similar to the HMO model, a space rented as accommodation may also violate a lender's mortgage, so check this first and make sure you're on the up and up. If the owner gives you the thumbs up, you're ready to go! Almost. As you might expect, rented accommodation requires the right location. Holidaymakers and business travellers will not be interested in booking a stay at a place that's out of the way from their primary focus. If the property isn't in a popular location with easy access to the city and transportation, it will be difficult to fill.

Because of the nature of an accommodation rental, there's a bit more in the way of service to think about. Accommodation spaces are almost always fully furnished, including general home appliances like microwaves, toasters, coffee makers, and sometimes even washing machines and dryers. Fully furnishing the accommodation is up to you. You'll want to make sure you offer just about every accoutrement a hotel would. This means a comfortable bed and plenty of fresh linen and towels. Your guest should have a well-equipped kitchen and bathroom, and a comfortable living space to relax or work. A desk or worktop is highly recommended, as the bulk of your guests will be professionals travelling. You'll also need to ensure the property is "turned over" properly between guests. Whether you do it yourself or hire a cleaner, the property should be cleaned from top to bottom in every room. Think of what would be expected from a hotel and do that. This is going to require a bit more management than the other two models.

Next, you should consider your marketing strategy. This is going to require a much different approach than the other two models, as well. As the property will be rented on a short-term basis, you'll need to keep your marketing fresh and relevant to avoid gaps between guests. Marketing like this can cost a bit more, so figure this into your budget.

General upkeep and maintenance of the space and its utilities will be another cost that differs a bit from the other two models. As I mentioned, guests of an accommodation space can tend to treat the space more aggressively than if it was their own residence. Build into your plan a regular assessment of the space and quickly fix anything that compromises the value of the space. Dents, windows, carpets, plumbing and electrical work; all of these should be checked as part of the turnover process. Keep the space fresh and inviting. Because there will be a much higher turnover of tenants, maintenance and upkeep may cost a bit more.

In a typical sublet, you're able to screen your prospects. In a short-term accommodation scenario, a background check is not common, and if it is done, it's generally not as thorough as it would be for an AST or HMO tenant. You lose a bit of control this way and take a slightly bigger risk with the legitimacy of your guests. On the other hand, if you get a rowdy or messy guest, they'll be gone soon. As part of the agreement you make with the subletter, you can create stipulations and parameters to mitigate this, such as disallowing the tenant to have overnight guests or disallowing pets.

With all this in mind, there is a very big benefit to subletting an accommodation space: profit. This model can theoretically bring you the most profit the fastest. The expected market cost for accommodations per day or week is generally much higher than the cost per day or week works out to in an AST or HMO scenario. Your prices are now in competition with other local hotels, motels, and bed and breakfast accommodations. This can quickly add up, and so long as you avoid gaps between guests, you can easily make a higher profit. Just remember that you'll incur additional costs furnishing and maintaining the unit between guests so figure this into your plan.

Personal Preparation

Now you've started to get an overview of what's involved in building a rent-to-rent business for yourself, but there's still a way to go yet. Will you be able to make it to the finish line? This isn't the kind of business you can set and walk away from with the expectation that it will operate on its own. You're seeing it does take effort, especially in place of money when you're starting without much (or any) capital. What else is it going to take from you to make this business grow and succeed? Do you have what it takes or can you get it? Now let's take a look at some of the key qualities and traits that will be required of you if you are to launch a rent-to-rent business with a drive to grow.

Time

It should be clear by now that this kind of business is not passive. You'll need to be involved in probably a daily basis in one respect or another. In many cases, time can be the most difficult commodity you sacrifice, especially if your rent-to-rent business is a side business to another job you're already accountable for. This is perhaps the largest personal preparation you'll need to undertake. Particularly at the onset of your business, you'll need to make time to get the business going, plan your strategy and business goals, negotiate, market your unit, and to manage your tenants and space. If you're hoping to grow quickly, you need additional time to accomplish this with more than one property. You may already be confident in your ability to manage your time properly, but here are a few tips to keep in mind as you begin:

Prioritise what needs to be done first or with utmost urgency. When you're first starting out, there will be a host of business setup steps and these should not be skipped, but some can fall lower on the list. Decide what needs to be done to get the ball rolling legally and work on your expansion and business identity as you go. Once you've completed the steps to setting up your business, you won't have to do those things again, and you'll get a good portion of your time back, which you can then use to complete some of the other, lesser tasks.

Break large tasks into smaller tasks you can accomplish in about an hour or two. All of the steps in front of you can seem daunting, but if you break them into smaller steps they are more manageable throughout your day or your week. For example, there are several steps involved in negotiating, but rather than think about everything you need to do to sign a contract with your property owner, focus on just one step. Find a contract template that suits the situation. That's one. You could theoretically do that in about 20 minutes online on https://www.LawDepot.co.uk. Edit the contract

to fit your business model. That's two. It can
probably be done in under an hour. Meet with your
property owner to go over the final details. That's
three. Instead of planning a whole day to take out
of your schedule and accomplish this, it may be
much easier for you to do one step each day. It may
not feel as though you're moving fast enough, but it
will be more manageable, less stressful, and you
know in your mind each small step brings you that
much closer to your goal.

Don't guess at what's next to be done; make yourself
a business roadmap. Outline all the steps you need
to take to get one subletter into a unit under your
rent-to-rent business and mark out on your calendar
or diary when you need (or want) them to be
completed by. Be easy on yourself and allow for
adjustments in the roadmap. When you've
completed those steps, make a new or expanded
roadmap from which to work next.

Avoid time-wasting activities and individuals when
you can. Interruptions are inevitable, but if you see
a friend call to chat while you know you should
really be completing a business step, let them go to
your voicemail and return the call when you
can. You'll have to get a bit selfish with your time,
and you should not feel guilty about it. These are
the practices you need to embrace to accomplish
your goals, and ultimately, to be able to spend more

time with the ones you love. By branching out and developing your rent-to-rent business, you're ultimately creating a stronger financial foundation for yourself, which will allow you to more easily spend time with those you love in the long run.

Delegate when you can. While you have a relatively small portfolio its quite manageable to do everything yourself. As you grow, it is essential to look for help. Property managers can sometimes be expensive, but you can strike a good relationship with a handyman or tradesperson that you trust, you can offer them a small percentage per room/property they fill, usually 7-11%. You can often find professional virtual assistants to help you on sites like Fiverr.com or Freelancer.com to help with any admin, bookkeeping or advertising and designing tasks. These tasks can usually be completed at a very low rate because many of the freelance workers on these sites are international and work for a lower cost per hour or per job than you might find in your own backyard. Websites can be created on Fiverr.com to a professional standard for as low as £100, depending on your requirements, and a logo for as little as £5. Though these tasks would be outsourced, the quality of the work remains acceptable because these virtual assistants regularly perform these tasks and understand what's expected despite not being local. If even a low monetary compensation is not in your budget, you can often find apps and programs (even free ones) that automate parts of your process for

you. For example, if you plan to run an email
marketing campaign for your rent-to-rent business,
rather than sending out hundreds of emails yourself,
set up a free automated email account, such as
reply.io and MailChimp, that will send these emails
for you at your specified dates and times. Some of
these systems can even be programmed to send
response emails when you receive interest from
prospects. Take time-consuming tasks off of your
list and put them onto the lists of robots or other
professionals via delegation.

Don't cancel appointments on yourself. When you
put a task into your diary, but there's no one else to
be accountable to, it's very easy to cancel your
appointment. Don't. Think of a time when you
may have put into your diary an appointment to go
to the gym in the morning. When the alarm goes
off, you're still sleepy, and no one is waiting for you
to show up, it's pretty easy to turn the alarm off and
roll back into your warm bedsheets. Don't allow this
to happen with the self-appointments you set for
your rent-to-rent business. Though you might not
have a direct person to be accountable to other than
yourself, there are ways to prompt your own
accountability. Search for free apps that help you to
stay on task and accountable to yourself, such as
Asana or Stickk. Better yet, use social media to find
yourself a mastermind group to join for
entrepreneurs, or even more specifically, property

management entrepreneurs. These kinds of support groups often have accountability processes built in because you're definitely not the only one facing this challenge. If you know you'll have to report back to your mastermind group with the results of the day, you may be more apt to do them.

Take time to rest. This may sound counterproductive, but burnout is a significant problem. At first, it may feel overwhelming with all you need to get done, but do not sacrifice the time you need to rest and recuperate. You will regret it. If you work yourself ragged, you risk burning out and cutting corners, and that's a poor way to start. Schedule some downtime and take it. The list of tasks will still be there for you when you get back, and they'll be much easier (and more fun) to handle when you've given yourself appropriate downtime.

Accountability

If you've made the time, but don't hold yourself accountable, you've still got some personal development to work on if you're to be successful in this endeavour. It's going to be crucial for you to set tasks and goals for yourself and your business and take responsibility for their completion. Even if you delegate tasks to others, you are still the one ultimately responsible for them. This is why it's a good idea to seek out an application that will keep you on task. My favourite accountability tool right now is Asana, and the reason I love it is that it syncs with my calendar and integrates with a number of time management tools, such as TimeDoctor, which tracks how much time I spend working on each task. I can assign tasks and deadlines to myself and others, and it includes a wide variety of task management features. A tool like this will make your business life much easier. I don't have to fumble with paper notes to myself or wonder what I need to do next, because the app tells me every day what's on my to-do list. You can even make your business roadmap inside this tool. Set dates, hold all of your project documentation and links there; it really does everything you need and it's free! Even if this tool isn't your first choice, there's a wide market of them available to select from. Find one and implement it.

Emotional Control

Things aren't always going to go your way and people aren't always going to do what you want, but it's important to keep your composure. This is true in any entrepreneurial path, but since your rent-to-rent business will involve a fair amount of negotiating, you should sharpen this skill now. Your body language is very revealing whether you're aware of it or not. Your posture, gestures, facial expressions, and breathing are all telling others what you're thinking and feeling even if your words aren't saying it. If you're not already familiar with how to use these aspects of yourself to communicate deliberately, then it's worth a brush-up. Though you may not feel confident negotiating and signing your very first deal, you want to give the impression you are. Though you may not feel like an experienced authority on rent-to-rent opportunities at the start, you want to act and sound as if you are. Believe it or not, these methods of communication can make or break your deal. Studies reveal that over fifty percent of an individual's first impression and opinion of another is based on body language and appearance alone. Only about five percent of an individual's impression of another is based on the words and verbal language communicated.

When you interact with prospective property owners and tenants, be cognizant of your posture. Stand straight with your shoulders back. Make eye contact. Smile. When the prospective client nods, you nod. Take notice of whether your shoulders are squarely facing the prospect or whether they are turned away. The same principle goes for the direction your feet are facing. If your shoulders and feet are facing an exit, for example, it gives the subconscious impression that you're looking for a way out; an escape.

Though it may sound strange, well-regulated breathing makes a significant subconscious impression on your prospects as well. Even if you're nervous, practise slow and steady breathing through your nose during your interaction. It's said that the person in the room with the most control is the one with a steady and calm breathing pattern. These practices may not come naturally at first, but give them some practice in other areas of your life. Practice deliberate body communication when you're in line at the market, when you speak to teachers or coaches, or even with your taxi driver. Make an effort to communicate deliberately and to keep cool under pressure.

Beyond your own body and verbal communication, be aware of theirs. Paying attention to the cues of your prospect will give you insight into how they're feeling and what they're thinking and this can help you build a rapport with them, and even anticipate their questions and decisions. For example, when an individual puts a hand to their face or chin in a gesture of consideration or contemplation, it's generally understood (at least subconsciously) that the individual is making an internal decision, or trying to. However, pay attention to the individual's eyes when this is happening. If the individual is looking straight ahead or even at you, there is no consideration happening internally, and their mind is likely already made up, and probably not in your favour. But if the individual is looking downward, a true consideration of your offer is happening internally. It will benefit you to become familiar with the basics of body language communication so that you can gain insight into the emotions and thoughts of your prospect. Utilise deliberate communication for yourself, and be looking for it in others as you move through your interaction.

Resilience and Adaptability

As is the case in many business pursuits, it helps tremendously to be open and flexible to change. Plans change all the time; priorities shift; deadlines change. Sometimes the prospect you were sure of closing gets cold feet at the last moment. You almost have to expect it and be ready to pivot your plan as needed so you will not slow your momentum. If you have your prime candidate lined up, have a backup candidate as well so you can quickly switch directions and go with another choice at a moment's notice. Make a business plan and roadmap for yourself but don't be afraid to adapt it at any time. While you might first think to change your plans is a sign of poor planning on your part, it's not. Holding tight to a rigid plan with no room for change is the weakness. It can actually be a sign of a strong business to change and adapt regularly. It's a demonstration of your drive and mastery to be able to amend plans and bounce back when things change.

Learn

well on your way to becoming a professional rent-to-rent business owner and you've already learned much, there's always more to learn and improve upon. Is it in your nature to want that continued learning? Here, you're getting a handle on the fundamentals, but if you're planning to run this business for a while yet, and to grow beyond rent-to-rent, there are many other aspects to become proficient in. The fundamentals in this crash course are solid, but it doesn't hurt to learn the same basics from another source. You'll be able to pick up on nuances, different perspectives, and different ways of operating. You may even notice some information repeats across sources; this can be a sign of details or information you don't want to compromise, and instead, build into your process as tried and true methods and ideas. Continuously put yourself in a learning situation. Join free (or paid) webinars online. Take a class or find a mentor. There are plenty of ways to ensure you're always learning, and thus, always drawing new power from learned information.

Passion for Growth

Rent-to-rent is where you start; it's not where you stop. If you truly plan to keep your business alive, you must plan for it to grow. This often means taking your rent-to-rent profit and eventually securing a property you can own and rent out. Though it doesn't always mean going from renter to owner on units.

In some cases, a rent-to-rent business owner doesn't plan to do anything in the way of property ownership. But this doesn't mean stop growing. There are plenty of ways to remain strictly rent-to-rent and still have a passion to grow and thrive. Scaling your business should always be in the business plan, whether your steps to growth are humble or grand.

In this first section, you've already gained a great deal of information on the business of subletting. You understand what rent-to-rent is and who's a part of it. You've examined the primary risks and benefits of starting a rent-to-rent business. It's now becoming clear to you what it will take, personally, to succeed at this type of business. Best of all, you've learned the three basic rental models and how each of these operates.

With all the information you've accrued so far, you should be able to begin making decisions about your business. In the next section, we'll take a look at a few more fundamental lessons and then I'll show you how to start using this information to make a strategy that will get the momentum going toward your enterprise.

Chapter 2:

Setting a Business Foundation

Now you're picking up speed. You've developed your overall understanding of the world of subletting. In this section, we'll begin to dig into the core components of this business. There are a few more basic concepts to cover before we take steps to set up your business for action. It's critical to understand the laws and restrictions of rent-to-rent. Nothing will take you down faster than trying to squeeze by this step. Learn the laws, use them, and follow them. This is one of the cornerstones you cannot do without. This is paramount to protecting yourself and your business.

I'll also help you to select a rental model, to begin with, and show you how to establish your budget and bandwidth for that model. We'll take a look at who uses these models and why it makes a good choice. If you truly have no money to begin, you may want to consider a borrowing plan that fits into your business model and your budget. I've had to take these steps myself to begin, and I'll walk you through my mistakes so you don't make the same ones. When you're finished with this section, we will have built an outline for your 12-month business plan and the annual goals that will keep your business growing at a healthy rate. Let's begin by examining the moral and ethical implications of the rent-to-rent business.

The Ethical Middleman

In the time that rent-to-rent business schemes have grown in popularity, they've also received a growing number of moral and ethical concerns. In this section, I'll reveal to you the four most concerning issues that continue to come up any time rent-to-rent subletting is discussed. These are the major concerns you need to be familiar with. I encourage you to make ethical choices in your business practice. What goes around, comes around.

Subletting Without Landlord Permission or Licencing

One of the biggest ethical concerns with subletting is deception. If you rent accommodation from a landlord or property owner with the intention to sublet, but you don't get the written okay to do so, you're causing a whole host of problems for every party involved, including yourself. If you sublet without permission from the property owner, you run the very real risk of being immediately removed from the process. Not only that, but the poor unfortunate subletter can also be removed. If the property owner does not own the property outright, but rather pays a mortgage, your sublet activity may very well be a violation of the mortgage. You could essentially get the property owner's property taken away from them. If it's not a violation of the mortgage, or there is no mortgage, it could still be a violation of the property owner's insurance, and that still causes for your removal and the subletter's.

Even if the landlord owns the property outright and there's no mortgage to pay, subletting could still be a violation of the insurance property and the policy could be dropped. You'll be lucky if it's only the property owner that comes after you in court. Watch what you tried to build go down in flames.

While subletting on one or two properties may not require a licence for your business, three or more will require it in England and Wales. If you seek to make a substantial profit, chances are you'll need three or more properties to sublet. It's best to get your licence while in the process of business setup, then you won't need to worry about it when you get the ball rolling on properties. Waiting can slow you down and cause you to miss out on a prime opportunity you find. If you try to circumvent these rules, you could be seeing your personal property taken from you in reparation. Be honest and upfront with your property owners and housing authorities. There are plenty of legitimate opportunities out there that won't require shady business. In short, don't even try it. It's not worth the risk.

Renting to Illegal Immigrants

Another shady practise often found in the business of rent-to-rent is subletting to individuals that do not have legal permission to enter or live in the UK. It's an unfortunate issue, but a very real one; more and more individuals enter the UK without first going through the proper channels whether for work, education, a better quality of life, or even asylum. These individuals and families still need a place to live, and it's here that the dishonest business person awaits their prey. A scenario like this looks like an easy benefit to the corrupt rent-to-rent business owner because you can increase the cost of the unit to take advantage of people who are desperate for housing. Furthermore, the illegal immigrant can do little in the way of protecting themselves from fair rent and good management because they have no legal recourse.

This might sound like an excellent way to gain profit without risk to yourself, but consider this: five years in prison and unlimited fines. These are the penalties looking you in the face if you get caught renting to illegal immigrants. So, what defines an illegal rent such as this? Anything that leads you to believe the individual or party does not have permission to enter or stay in the UK or if that permission has expired. Falsified or even incorrect documentation of permission from these individuals is also included. You run the very real risk of facing these penalties if there's any reason to believe your subletter is illegal. In such a situation, don't expect the property owner to take the fall. If you've sublet, even with your landlord's permission, to an illegal immigrant, it is you who will face the civil penalties.

Trustworthy business professionals will always officially check a tenant's right to rent. If you cannot prove that you've taken this step and documented your investigation, you'll almost certainly be fined. For any tenancy starting on or after 2014 (or 2016 in some areas), you'll need to perform this check before finalising your contract and move-in date with your tenants. To investigate this and document your investigation, the housing authorities require that you ask your prospective tenant for original, genuine, documentation and that you save copies of that documentation at least 28 days before the tenancy begins. Even if an adult tenant is not listed on the lease, but still resides at the location, you'll need to check. There are some cases in which you do not need to check, such as providing social housing or accommodations to refugees, but you'll always want to make sure you've got this base covered. For more specific information on these requirements, you can visit https://www.gov.uk and search for "check your tenant's right to rent", or "right to rent check". You'll be brought to various pages that outline in detail what's required, for who, and

when. You can even use the site to link to the
housing authorities, which provides an online
checking tool to help you. If you've taken these
steps, but you're still not sure what to do, your
safest bet is to contact local authorities to request
further guidance. Contact information is also found
on this site.

Surging Rent Costs

Profit. Profit. Profit. This is the goal. However,
some sublet businesses take advantage of the
opportunity to make a profit off of the ever-growing
need for housing, especially in London, Bristol, and
larger cities. To make a profit, as you're learning,
you'll need to charge a higher cost of rent to your
subletters than you're paying to your property
owner. This is usually done by striking a deal with
the property owner for a lower guaranteed rent than
the typical market value. Then, you'll generally
spike the rent to your subletter slightly to make up
for maintenance and management costs. But
"slightly" is the keyword. The legitimate rent-to-
rent business owner would theoretically investigate
the average market value for renting a unit in
whichever city or town the property is located in,
and then plan to sublet for a cost of something
within that general range.

The unprincipled rent-to-rent professional,

however, will raise the cost to the subletter by sometimes double or more. At first, you may wonder how it's possible to close deals with such a high cost, but the growing demand for housing leaves many desperate for space and with no other option but to comply with the costly rent or face homelessness. As this happens more and more, especially in populated cities, we see the market value on rental units surging. Rent-to-rent professionals who do this end up contributing to the growing problem of exorbitant rental costs and affect the local economy in a negative way. Though some individuals may be able to accept and absorb a higher rental cost, many cannot and it forces individuals to make less than desirable choices, like applying for social housing, to make ends meet. Average rental costs skyrocket. It's okay to raise the cost a bit, but price fairly and you'll keep tenants longer, and you won't be responsible for one of the plaguing social issues facing city housing today.

Non-Management

If spiralling rent cost isn't bad enough, many of the unscrupulous sublet businesses take a more than passive position and shirk the responsibility to maintain the property. These "slumlord middlemen" neglect repairs, internal and external repairs, utility management, waste and rubbish removal, and generally make the unit and the neighbourhood drop in value. Not to mention the effect it has on your tenant's quality of life. If you're planning on cutting corners and making a habit of unethical business practices, go ahead and plan for a swarm of trouble to follow you around until you straighten out your game and play nice.

The truth is that a respectable profit can be made legitimately and legally, and you don't have to sink so low to do it. For your business to last and grow, play fairly, do your due diligence, manage your clients, and care for your properties. As you're learning, rent-to-rent business is not passive, and it requires your attention and responsibility. It takes effort to manage your property, tenants, and property owners, and that's only after you've taken the time to market yourself and your units effectively. If you're willing to put in the work though, rent-to-rent can be exactly the footing you need to get you cruising in profitable property management.

What Not to Do

In my time working in both rent-to-rent and buy-to-rent capacities, I've seen many mistakes made, and I've made some myself. I will tell you from my own experience that these mistakes will cost you a good deal of time to repair and recover from and in some cases, time loss is not the only disadvantage you face. Next, we'll quickly roll through what *not* to do in your rent-to-rent business. Some of these mistakes are extensions of points we've already covered but they're worth going into detail and repeating. Let's take a look at what to avoid.

Using the Incorrect Agreements

Avoid getting lazy with your agreements. There is not one agreement to rule them all. The terms in each type of agreement are different and stipulate certain allowances and restrictions. It's possible to download and use standard company let agreements, but it's likely that as you get weeks and months into the rental, you'll find numerous points that haven't been clarified in your contract and you'll wish they were. This will result in your needing to get a new agreement signed part-way through the process, and this will not only take your time and effort, but it can also make you appear unprofessional or untrustworthy. Your property owner may become suspicious of this. Worse, the holes in your contract could be spotted by the property manager

themselves, and they will require a drawing up of a
new contract, or they may try to take advantage of
you. The contract between you and your property
managers should be clear about whether or not you
have permission to sublet, who is responsible for
what management and upkeep, who pays for what
and when, how long your agreement is, who and
how many individuals can occupy the residence, and
what kind of work can (or should) be done to the
unit.

In most sublet scenarios, the contract you form
between you and the property owners will likely not
vary too much. However, there will be differences
between subletting residential and commercial units.
Make sure you're using the correct version. Beyond
that, the terms will vary only slightly between you
and your property owners for sublets in a simple
situation, so you can probably draw up a contract for
residential and one for commercial and continue to
use the same contracts by making only the basic
changes per opportunity if you're starting with only
residential, or only commercial, even easier. It's
always better to keep it simple at the outset and
build on your success as you go.

Contractually, the biggest differences will occur
between you and your subletters, especially if you
plan to work with more than one sublet model. You
cannot use a standard let agreement to cover all

models. If you plan on using each model to make a profit, you need to draw up a contract for ASTs, one for HMOs, and one for accommodations. You cannot use a standard AST contract for HMO model, as all of the relevant clauses need to be added to relate to subletting. I highly recommend getting a solicitor to write up your contracts - there are numerous examples online, such as https://www.LawDepot.co.uk, but cutting corners could come back to haunt you. You could always find a contract you could always get a solicitor to read over it and amend it for you if necessary.

In some cases, you may even need a different contract depending upon who you're subletting to. For example, if you and your property owner should so choose to offer social housing, different rules apply. Once you decide on which model(s) you'll use to start your business, which types of properties you're planning to sublet, and to whom, you'll form a small collection of perhaps a half-dozen contracts. Keep these close to hand and pull out the appropriate agreement when you need it. As you grow, you'll refine your process and your agreements and in fact making these revisions should be a part of your 12-month business plan.

Skipping Licencing, Rules, and Business Insurance

I've said it before, and it's worth repeating, *do not*

skip the step of legitimising your sublet business. When you set out, you need to register your business. It's highly unsafe for you to start subletting without this both legally and financially. Similarly, you need to ensure your business. If you don't and something negative occurs, it will be your personal assets that are taken.

Depending on where your business operation is located, and where your rental units are located, business rules can vary. It's important to become familiar with the requirements in your area(s) so you know what operations break the rules and how to avoid them. If you are renting an office from which you work, it will be a different set of requirements than if you work from your own residence. You may even be required to pay business rates, and you may qualify for a deduction of business expenses, which is something definitely worth registering your business for.

If you plan to take on others to help you, whether it be an official employee, an agent, or even in some cases a freelancer, there are several related regulations with which to comply. As you might expect, an official employee is going to require a greater amount of upfront work. For this reason, many rent-to-rent professionals hold off on employing others until they're sure the business is stable. For example, adding employees to your business will likely require you to meet minimum wage, ensure the individual has the right to work in the UK, ensure the individual has no criminal record, register as an employer, and ensure you provide all the necessary accommodations to employees such as a pension plan. The official https://www.gov.uk site outlines all of these requirements and provides details on how to go about all of them. If you are planning on employing others, don't wait until the last minute to take these steps. It's often the case that this takes time, especially going back and forth with officials in the start so you should give yourself a solid month or more to establish these requirements.

Lastly, do not skip proper licencing for the type of sublet model you use. While an AST sublet may not require additional licencing, an HMO or accommodation model will, due to the type of residency. For example, housing authorities want to make sure that if you sublet to multiple separate individuals in one unit, you're doing it in a way that's safe for the tenants. When tenants share common areas, you need to follow a strict set of rules; you can't just go converting kitchens into rooms. The licencing of an HMO sublet business is meant to ensure you know what those rules are and that you follow them. In almost every case, it's you the middleman that needs to apply for this licence. Don't just assume it's the property owner's responsibility. If you are found to be operating an

HMO sublet without the correct licence, you and possibly even the property owner will be prosecuted. The rules and regulations are quite clear. Follow them. The fines and punishments are too great to ignore this step. Especially in the case of beginning this business with little to no capital, you cannot afford the penalty. Your entire profit, and likely your assets, will be lost to compensate for skipping this step. Beyond that, you could entirely lose your right to operate as a business altogether.

Subletting for the Entire Term of Your Lease

I've made this mistake myself. It's an easy trap to fall into if you're not aware of it. When you sublet, do not write your sublet contract for the same timeframe of the lease you signed with your property owner. You sublet tenancy should be for at least one day less than the agreement you've set with your property owner. Failing to do so can result in an unscrupulous property owner swooping in on your tenant and collecting the rent you've set, but leaving all the work for you.

Neglecting the Terms and Conditions of the Mortgage or Insurance

Earlier, I mentioned the downfalls of this, but it's another worth repeating. Some mortgages, as well as some insurance policies, include stipulations about letting and subletting, mostly because it opens the door for more damage to the property. For example, some mortgages or policies do not allow for subletting as an HMO or restrict the amount of time in which a property can be leased as an AST. Neglecting these rules can very easily result in the property being repossessed or the insurance policy being dropped. Though the mortgage and the insurance policy may be in the name of the property owner, it's still you - the one who takes the sublet action - that's responsible for this neglect. In such a case, now it's not only the housing authority that will come after you, but it's also probably the property owner, too. In every property you lease from a property owner, check thoroughly through the terms and conditions for both the mortgage and the insurance policy. In some cases, rare ones, the property owner may be willing to make a change to a lender or insurance company that offers a looser agreement that will benefit you both.

As a side note, it pretty much goes without saying, you should not violate the terms of your lease with the property owner, as well. If there's a stipulation in your lease that disallows you to sublet, do not sublet. If your lease makes no mention of whether or not you can sublet, ask. Basically, always ask and get it in writing, that your property owner is allowing you to sublet.

Skipping the Right to Rent Background Check

In most every sublet scenario, it's the middleman's responsibility to perform the check to ensure your prospective tenant has the legal right to live in the UK. Letting to an illegal immigrant is a serious offence that can land you substantial fines at best, and criminal conviction with up to five years in prison in the worst case. Either penalty will stop your business dead. Do not forego this step before finalising your sublet agreement.

Determining Your Most Viable Rental Model

Moving forward, it's time to decide which is the most viable rental model for you to begin with. Finances will have a lot to do with this decision. Which model can you afford to begin? Your bandwidth for management will also play a large part in decision-making at this point. HMOs and accommodation units will almost certainly require more work in management, but your profit will almost certainly be more.

For this reason, this is the method that I prefer, and when the workload gets too much to manage, or you want to make your income stream truly passive, you can always hire a property manager. Finally, your decision should take into account your business growth strategy. Will you be sticking with one model for the entire year, or do you plan to take on other models as you grow?

The Financial Decision

One of the benefits that have probably drawn you to the idea of rent-to-rent initially is the idea that you can begin this business with very little capital, and under the right circumstances, none at all. This is very true, but it does take your understanding to select the wisest model to start. If you're starting

with little to no money to invest, ASTs are going to
be the simplest and least expensive way to begin.
It's relatively easy to find properties that are ready to
go as an AST rental. So long as your agreement
with your property owner is on the up-and-up in
terms of subletting, and the mortgage and insurance
permit it, it's effort and time you'll need to invest
and not money. However, business licencing,
business insurance, and other initial setup
requirements could cost you, so plan for this in your
initial budget. I've already made it perfectly clear
that this is not a step you can skip, but this is the
time when it's most tempting. If you truly have
nothing to start with, consider various types of
borrowing. It's possible to use a line of credit, or a
small business loan to defray your start-up costs
until you're pulling in a profit.

In many cases, if your credit is strong enough, you
may even be able to get a line of credit or a loan that
offers 0% interest for a period of time (usually 6
months) if you've repaid by then. Six months is
ample time to collect enough profit to repay what
you borrowed to start your business. Either way,
with little start-up capital, an AST model will be the
best choice. If other models are what you're aiming
for, consider starting with a few AST properties and
branching out as you gain momentum and
money. It is possible to find units that are ready to
go as HMOs or accommodations, but these almost

always cost more to manage, not to mention to begin, as they require more licencing.

If you're starting out with some amount of capital, consider if it's enough to start with an HMO, because this is almost certainly where your greatest profit will be made. If you're setting out with a healthy start-up capital, ask yourself why you're turning to rent-to-rent instead of buy-to-rent models. While it's true that rent-to-rent can take some of the pressure off of you, it likely does not outweigh the benefits. Owning to rent is going to place you in more control and it's going to give you capital growth over time; two huge benefits. Not to mention, if you start as the owner, you are in a position to collect a guaranteed rent and pass the work onto a subletter if you so choose.

Even though I do now own multiple Buy to Let properties as well, it is just too easy to make money from the rent to rent model, so I am still always looking to invest in new opportunities. The main reasons for this are the quick turnaround and the fact that I don't need to outlay the capital for a £40,000 deposit or the astronomical fees involved with Buy to Let.

The Management Decision

As mentioned previously, any of these models are going to take work to manage. Your tenants need attention, and your units need care. No matter what, there will be work to do to set up your business initially. The question is, how much time do you have and how much work can you manage? The longer it takes to set up your business, the longer it takes to make a profit, because you can't-what? Skip this step.

If you plan to manage multiple units, you need to compound the amount of time and effort it's going to take. If this will be your only work, that's one thing, but if you have another part-time or full-time obligation, you'll need to be very proficient at time management. You can't afford to neglect the obligations of starting a business and maintaining tenants and properties. One of the most critical points to apply effort and time will be when sublet agreements are coming to an end. If you don't have the time to market, host viewings, and work negotiations, you'll find yourself having to pay guaranteed rent but not collecting any rent yourself. Letting it go for one month might be alright, but more than that and your quarterly profit starts to drop significantly while your costs still remain.

A couple of AST arrangements might be manageable, but consider the work involved in working an HMO with multiple tenants that need your attention. Further, if you've not done a thorough job of aligning tenants under one roof that get along amiably, you might have social drama to contend with and settling that can take additional time. HMOs, as you've seen, also run the possibility of more initial work upfront to ensure your unit is suitable for multiple tenants while still adhering to all local and national law. An accommodation unit can take the most work because you'll be required to turn over guests relatively quickly, and this includes an entire reset of the unit before the next guest arrives. If you don't have the money to delegate this to others, you'll have to do it yourself. If you cut corners and leave your new guest with lacklustre entry, the word soon gets out, and your bookings suffer.

That raises another point. Marketing is a very crucial part of your enterprise. Again, if you cannot delegate this responsibility, it's on you. If you don't make time for marketing, you're going to have a tough time finding subletters and guests for your units.

The time and effort it takes to start and manage a rent-to-rent business (or even a buy-to-rent business for that matter) is one of the most overlooked and neglected facets in the profession. This isn't necessarily even intended but happens when businesses don't take the time to

think and plan it out. Jumping into the business
and building momentum and profit quickly is
enticing, but without proper planning, time and
effort, you'll slow to a stop quickly. Time
management is easily the biggest showstopper for a
new rent-to-rent business. Plan wisely and avoid the
sudden stop.

The Growth Decision

Money, time, and effort are important, but your
business growth plan may be the most important to
consider when selecting a sublet model to start
with. This is last on the list because money, time,
and effort all play a part in this decision. However,
if you start your business without having this plan in
place, it will be extremely difficult to measure your
results and success. If you don't have an end goal in
mind, at least for the year, you'll just be floating in a
sea with no destination and no motor to get you
there. Honestly, collecting a profit's great, but what
real good is it for your business if you're not using it
to grow?

It seems rather obvious the more profit you make,
with a model like an HMO or accommodation unit,
and the faster you make it, the faster you grow, but
not if you don't have a plan for growth. It's very
common for a professional to begin with a few
AST-style properties and as profit comes in and

costs are mitigated and defrayed, that profit is invested into an HMO or accommodation unit. It's also very common for that profit to be put toward a buy-to-rent opportunity so that the property's capital growth is yours. Each of these will require more money and more time, especially if you begin to delegate aspects of your obligations.

My advice to you is to run the general numbers and find something that's manageable and easily affordable, even leaving you with room to wiggle. As you get closer to the time when you can expand, and you've got your eye on a few prospective units to help you do so, run the numbers again, this time more specifically. What will it take to invest in a more profitable sublet model and by what point do you expect to start that expansion? Six months? Nine months? A year? Two? There's no wrong answer except not planning. Make a benchmark for yourself and don't hesitate to refine this plan as you go. It's really the only way you'll know if you're on track for growth, and if not, what needs to change to get you back on track. When you have a general outline for growth over 12 months, it will make choosing a sublet model quite easy.

If you've taken these steps and you're still having trouble deciding where to start, start small and simple; start with an AST model. It will allow you to get the hang of the business quickly and to project the amount of time and money it will

require to take on a bigger project like an HMO or
accommodation model.

It's worth mentioning at this point that ASTs,
HMOs, and accommodation units are not the only
models for subletting. Another model you'll find,
though less common for a rent-to-rent business is
letting to a lodger.

The Lodging Model

Let's assume for a moment that you reside under a
common AST model, or even in a home you already
own. Let's also assume, too, that you haven't the
capital, and maybe even the time, to dedicate to
subletting. You still want to make some form of
profit. Offering lodging might be a solid temporary
solution to get you off the ground and into the
world of profitable subletting.

The lodging model is a simple one with few
regulations, though the regulations that do exist are
still just as important to adhere to. Whether you're
a tenant of a landlord's AST property or you own
your own home, you still need to ensure your ability
to take in a lodger. As a tenant, you need to make
sure your landlord will allow you to have a lodger.
As an owner, you need to ensure you don't violate
mortgage or insurance terms by taking in a lodger.

What's the difference between a lodger and a subletter? Mostly, control. A subletter has a right to their own room, and the landlord (including you) cannot enter without permission. You also cannot dictate (to an extent) how the subletter uses that room. A lodger, on the other hand, doesn't hold that control. You can enter a lodger's room as it is essentially still your room. A lodger must still have access to kitchen and bathroom facilities within the property, however. There are a few other stipulations to be familiar with in a lodging situation, such as offering to lodge to a family member or offering to lodge in a unit that's already part of social housing. There are regulations for the income made from a lodging room and the taxes you're subject to, as well as credits. Lodging, like any of these models, will require that the entire unit (not just the room) is up to code, safe, and provides necessary utilities and accommodations. You'll also still be responsible for a Right to Rent check. If you're considering a lodging unit as your starting point, visit https://www.gov.uk for the specifics in your area and for your specific situation. A lodging model is going to be the least profitable model to use, but if it's all you can manage, it might be better than nothing at all. But keep in mind, now you have to share a space with your lodger and this might impinge on your own quality of life.

Your 12-Month Business Plan and Annual Growth Goals

Sometimes start-up businesses don't make a 12-month plan at the outset. Let this be another of my own mistakes you learn from and avoid. I didn't have a business plan in year one or year two, and it really slowed my growth. Sure, I was making a profit, but I was spinning my wheels on where to go next and burning money on how to get there. I had no orientation on how to get to what's next because I had no plan. At the end of the fourth quarter in year two, I decided enough was enough, and it was time to get serious. I spent most of October and November building my written business plan for the upcoming 12 months. The success and confidence I experienced in year three was an exceptional difference. Have that exceptional success for yourself in year one. Make a 12-month business plan complete with goals for your business growth.

There are three common types of written business plans:

Working Business Plan - A rough internal document that you work from and share with others inside the business. It's your business guideline, and it's used regularly to steer your ship. This plan is generally very descriptive to help your internal staff and yourself, but it's not necessarily beautiful. It's not necessarily something you'd want to present without formalising it.

Abbreviated Business Plan - Whereas formal business plans can be upwards of twenty pages long; an abbreviated plan is about 1-5 pages in length. It includes most or all of the complete formal version, but typically not as much detail is provided in each section. This version of your business plan is typically used when trying to get help from lenders or investors and the like, so it should be a presentable copy that's clear for all who read it.

A Formal Business Plan - A full and complete business plan ready for any audience you wish to share it with. This version of your business plan can be as long as 10 or 20 pages and includes all the typical sections of a business plan in detail, including financial records and other formal documentation. This can be used for lenders and investors, but keep in mind that sometimes these parties are more interested in the abbreviated plan.

It's hard to compose, and even harder to follow, a 12-month business plan if you're not sure what it is or how to use it. Your business plan should clearly describe your business, its components, its goals, and its plans to reach those goals. A business plan also often includes legal business documentation and financial records, but this is more so the case in abbreviated or formal presentation plans with and external receiving audience.

There's an old idea that a 12-month business strategy is more about the planning and less about the plan. What's meant by that is the process of sitting down to write out the sections of a business plan forces you to think about aspects of your business you may not have considered so that when that part of the plan arrives, or better yet when an unforeseen circumstance arises, you've got a guideline on how to operate and still aim toward your goals.

It's important to remember your 12-month business plan is a living document. Remember when I mentioned adaptability and resilience? The business plan is a perfect example of where to apply that quality, especially at year one. The document will change and grow in order to overcome challenges, obstacles, and shifting goals. It's not a rigid dictation of exactly what must happen or else, and in fact, it's unhealthy for your business to treat it as such.

The major mistake made with a 12-month rent-to-rent business plan is the amount of time and effort put into it. It's often too much or too little time. Keep your audience in mind when making your plan. Will you be showing it to investors or using it internally? The level of time and detail you put into it will be affected by whether the document is meant to be presented or used as a guide internally. While you certainly want to spend more than a day to create your business plan, you probably don't want to spend more than a month making it, or it's taking up too much of your time. If start-up capital isn't a problem for you, you can often find freelance professionals who can draw up your business plan for you. When you make your initial 12-month plan, you want to aim for somewhere between a working plan and an abbreviated plan (unless you plan to seek out investors and the like) and it should be about 3-5 pages in length. Remember to back up your plans with metrics, numbers, and projections.

So what goes into a business plan? A business plan doesn't necessarily need to follow a certain format, but it should include certain information and sections. Let's take a look:

Executive Summary

This is typically at the start of the document, and it includes a description of your rent-to-rent business; the business concept and the mission statement. This part of the document is meant to give those reading it a general understanding of how the business operates. This typically explains the day-to-day business functions, the location and surrounding environment of the business, and the people involved in performing regular tasks for the business.

Financial Status and Strategy

This section of the 12-month business plan can vary
a bit depending on whether your business is new
and just starting or whether you're several years into
the business. If you're new, this section typically
includes a breakdown of the start-up costs you
anticipate, that business capital you currently have or
want to establish, usually through a borrowing
plan. This section should also include a projected
cash flow statement and a profit-and-loss statement.
Great plans will also include a break-even analysis
that describes how your business plans to at least
break even if no significant profit is made over the
course of 12 months. This is more important to
include if you seek to borrow money and you're
presenting this business plan to lenders or investors.

Marketing Strategy

While this section is often more significant for
businesses selling a product, it's still important to
include it, though it doesn't have to be as long as a
business plan that includes sold products at a brick-
and-mortar location or via eCommerce. In this
section, you should include a description of how you
plan to market your properties online and/or in the
community. This could include any social media

marketing plans, Google Ads, the viewing and negotiation process, and even networking strategies, which is part of any successful rent-to-rent business.

Customer Analysis

This section of your business plan should include a breakdown of the customer base you intend to serve. Describe your primary customer; your ideal customer; your target customer. If you plan to serve one sort of customer during the start of the year, but you plan to expand or shift to another sort of customer within your 12-month period, explain that as well. If you can, describe your customer's median income and what that customer is used to paying for your services in your area.

Competition Analysis

This section should include a profile of the competition and their services, the amount of competition in your region, and the median cost for their services. Describe what the competition does for marketing, the length of time the average competition has been operational in your region, and probably most importantly, how you plan to compete. Find what sets you apart from the competition and makes your services unique. This will often be the number one way you get a leg up on the competition.

Industry Analysis

Your lenders, investors, and other interested
business parties may not always be familiar with the
industry or profession in which you work. Describe
to them in this section what the industry profile is.
Explain what the industry has looked like in your
region over the last five years and whether cost and
profit have increased or decreased. Include the
supply and demand for these industry services and
the expected projection for this over the next five
years.

SWOT Analysis

Perhaps one of the most important sections for you
to complete - for yourself - is a SWOT analysis. A
SWOT analysis is a comprehensive study of your
business' strengths and weaknesses; your
opportunities and threats. Taking time to write up
this portion of the business plan is often very
revealing and will allow you to spot concerns and
opportunities you may not have noticed without
performing this bit of work. It's a beneficial section
for the audience of your document, but this is
almost always more important to the business itself
as a planning tool. I highly recommend you
concentrate efforts on this section of your 12-month

business plan, and perhaps even start here and use what you find to determine other sections of your business strategy.

Contingency Plan

In this section of your document, you need to plan for worst-case scenarios. The contingency plan is used to prepare for an outcome that's unlikely, but disastrous if it should occur. Explain why the outcome would be a huge negative impact on your business. Describe how your business plans to mitigate these damages and repair them, should they occur.

Goals and KPIs

Goals and KPIs (Key Performance Indicators) are often a part of each relevant section, but usually, a 12-month business plan will dedicate an entire section to defining the milestone goals that will determine your success and growth. KPIs and other metrics are used to measure the success of each goal so that you can tell how much under or over your goal your business has performed. It also serves as an excellent gauge on the timeframe in which each of these goals is accomplished so you can tell if your projected timeframe is over, under, or right on target. Year over year, this part of your plan will serve as a crucial element in your growth. You'll be able to compare last year's goals and KPIs with the goals you set for the coming year.

Elevator Pitch

A 12-month business plan does not necessarily require the inclusion of your "elevator pitch", but this is an excellent exercise and inclusion for new businesses. Including a section for your elevator pitch will allow you to focus and refine the explanation of what your business does, in a way that others can understand in about 30 seconds or less.

If you're feeling overwhelmed, putting together a 12-month business plan for the first time, don't panic. Every business owner has been where you are now. It is tricky, but it's possible, and once you start in on the project it becomes easier. Better yet, it opens you up to a perspective on your business and its growth that you may likely not have seen. To make life easier, there are several software applications and business plan templates available online, both for free and for cost, that can help you to make this plan. There are videos online to walk you through the details. If you have the budget for it, there are services that will make your plan for you with your help and then review it with you to make sure you benefit from it as much as your audience will.

It can be overwhelming to draw up a 12-month business plan for the first time, but it's going to be much more difficult for you if you skip this step; take my word for it. Fortunately, your year two business plan will be easier for you. Your business start-up will be complete, so you won't need to cover that additional concept. You'll have already made one plan, so the second will be all the easier to manage. When you get to year two, you can compare your plan with the year one plan. Just think how easy next year's plan will be if you start now.

Chapter 3:

The Business Setup

You've essentially found yourself at the start of a fantastic job thus far! You've made it past the majority of the heavy-lifting concepts. You have a solid grip on which sublet model(s) you're interested in working with and hopefully you've chosen which to begin with first. You're aware of the risks and benefits associated with each and the legal regulations to which you should adhere. You know what a business like this is going to require from you in terms of money, time, effort, and personal characteristics. I've given you the five most common mistakes to avoid when starting your rent-to-rent business so that you can learn from them without making them. Best yet, you've developed an understanding of how to set yourself up with a comprehensive and insightful 12-month business plan to use as your guide through the next year and beyond. Now it's time to dive into the nitty-gritty and focus on the step-by-step actions you need to take to establish your rent-to-rent business so you can get yourself registered as a legal operation.

In this section, I'll help you to select a business structure (not to be confused with your sublet model) and gathering the appropriate documentation and contracts you'll need to conduct business. We'll take a quick look at what it means to become a part of a redress scheme for your business and how to protect the rights of your prospects as you collect personal information from them. We learned earlier that more than fifty percent of an individual's opinion of you is formed by your body language and appearance, and this is not much different for your business. Lastly, I'll run you through the basics of establishing your business locally and online so that it's easy for individuals to find your business, your available properties, and feel confident working with your business because of your professional image. Let's get started.

Select a Business Structure

There are three types of business structures that make sense for you to select from in order to start your small rent-to-rent business. As with anything, there are advantages and disadvantages to each. When you select one structure, it doesn't mean you're stuck with that forever. It's common for a business to start with one structure and to grow into another as your success grows. Let's get into it and see which structure will work best for your year one business.

Sole Trader Business Structure

A sole trader structure is the simplest and fastest to set up, but it carries the most risk. As a sole trader, you're a legal business but set up under your own personal identity. Any financial damage incurred is your personal responsibility to repair with your own financial assets. If another individual, business, or insurance company comes after you legally, it's you personally they come after and there's no way for you to deflect that to your business, since you personally are the business.

Limited Company Structure

A limited company structure allows you to set up your business separate from yourself so that if, heaven forbid, your business starts to head south, you are not personally responsible for these debts. It's a bit more work at the outset and you'll be responsible for following a stricter set of rules, but my personal recommendation is that these additional steps, rules, and costs are well worth it to protect your personal assets. As a limited company, you'll be responsible for formal documentation of company records and for updating any business structure changes you make throughout the year. If you have the budget, it often helps to hire an accountant to help with these additional responsibilities. If that's not in your budget, it's possible to do this yourself, but it will take you some extra time and effort. Fortunately, the internet is full of help and software applications to make this management easier. You'll also be required to file company tax returns and pay corporate taxes. Setting up as a limited company, but then not following these rules can result in fines, prosecution, and even disqualification of your business. Having a Limited Company can also have many tax benefits, especially the fact that the dividends tax bracket is lower than the PAYE income tax bracket, but it's worth speaking to a tax advisor or accountant for more information.

Partnership Structures

If you're starting your rent-to-rent business with at least one other interested party, a partnership structure may be your best choice. A partnership structure is the most complex of the three options, but as you might suspect, the available opportunities may be greater for you depending on your circumstances. It's important to note at this point that a partnership does not necessarily mean two (or more) individuals. A partnership can exist between two (or more) individuals, an individual and an existing limited company, or two (or more) limited companies. That is to say a limited company essentially counts as a 'legal person'.

There are also two different types of partnerships from which to select your structure: a limited partnership, and a limited liability partnership. The major difference between these two partnerships, for our intents at least, is the liability. In a limited partnership, both partners (whether limited company or individual) are personally responsible for debts incurred by the business partnership. However, each partner is personally responsible for debts only up to the amount of which that partner has contributed to the business. In a limited liability partnership, partners are better protected from personal liability.

However, the intricacies of partnership structures are greater. For example, in a limited partnership, one partner must be named the 'general partner' and the other party, or parties, should be listed as limited partners. The limited partner(s) are not able to take on as much business responsibility. A general limited partner is responsible for any debts the business is not able to pay, and they basically control and manage the business. The general partner is able to make binding business decisions, whereas the limited partner is not. The limited partner is only liable for the business debts up to the amount of which they've contributed to the business and they are not able to make as many business decisions, especially binding decisions. Partners split profits and pay taxes independently on what they've collected. Beyond liability and responsibility differences, and declaring general and limited partners, there are a few other things to keep in mind in the case of a partnership business establishment.

A limited partnership must include an official business address. You can use a PO Box address, but you still must register a main physical address from which business is conducted. This can be a home address, but note that this address will be publicly available. Also, note that your official business address must be in the same country that your partnership is registered in.

There are also stipulations as to what your business name can be. You do not have to register an official business name in the case of a limited partnership. You can trade under your own names,

but all partner names and the business name (if you
have one) must be included on all official documents
such as business documentation, business letters,
and invoices. A limited partnership establishment
must not use terms such as "limited liability
partnership" or "LLP", as it is technically not an
LLP. Your partnership business name cannot
include offensive or socially sensitive terms, and it
cannot be the same as an already existing trademark
business name. Your business name cannot suggest
your connection to government or local authorities
and it cannot use the term "accredited". There are
some exceptions to these business name rules, but
you must receive prior written permission from the
Company House in order to do so.

In the case of a limited liability partnership, you
must register a business address, and just like a
limited partnership, this address can be a PO Box,
but you must also register a physical address, and
this address must be the same. Again, it can be a
home address, but note that this address will be
available to the public.

A limited liability partnership does need to have an
official name; you cannot trade under your personal
identity alone. This business must include the term
"limited liability partnership" or "LLP" as part of
the name. This business name must be registered
with Companies House, the same as a limited

partnership should. Same as with a limited partnership, your business name must not suggest or use official terms without written permission and it must not be the same or too close to a similar name of an already existing business unless you have written consent from that entity to use it. If for some reason, you want to operate under a different business name than your official limited liability partnership name, you can, and you need not register that name, but it still needs to follow a few certain rules, such as, it cannot use the term "limited" or "LTD" in that name.

Similarly to the way a limited partnership must determine a general partner and a limited partner, a limited liability partnership must determine at least two "designated partners" which will be responsible for official business documentation, record-keeping, and decision-making. The other partners, should you have any, would be general partners. Designated partners are responsible for registering the business for Self-Assessment with HMRC, and they must also be individually registered for Self-Assessment themselves. If your rent-to-rent partnership plans to make greater than £85,000 a year, a designated partner must register the business for VAT, prepare, sign, and send annual accounts and confirmation statements to Companies House. Since designated members hold accountability, if they fail to comply with business requirements, they are subject to fines and prosecution.

If you make the decision to use a limited liability partnership and establish designated partners, because there must be at least two, it's important to take the extra step of creating an LLP agreement between those designated members in order to be clear about who does what, how profits will be shared, and how partners will join or leave the LLP.

Join the PRS

The PRS, or Property Redress Scheme, is authorised by the Department for Communities and Local Government ("DCLG") and by the National Trading Standards Estate Agency Team to help consumers with complaints and disputes in a rent-to-rent scenario. Since you are a middleman and service, both the property owner and the tenant, your position can be a precarious one, and you are not always the best individual to resolve these issues. If a complaint or dispute is raised to you from either the property owner or the tenant, you should, of course, seek to resolve the issue to your best, and unbiased, ability. However, this is not always an easy task, especially where your own profit is concerned. Instead, unresolved complaints from either the property owner or the tenant can be raised to the PRS for resolution if none has been found. The PRS acts as an independent and unbiased agency, and though the focus is to help the consumer, it's a huge help to you as well. Becoming a member of the PRS shows that your business is dedicated to excellent customer service for both your landlords and tenants. It also suggests that you care deeply about improving property industry standards in your region.

If a complaint is raised to the PRS, the process for resolution is a fairly simple one that is completed within 40 days from the time of the complaint.

Members (that would be you) are given the opportunity to resolve the complaint first. If that doesn't work, the PRS acts as a mediator to try to come to a fair agreement for all. And if that doesn't work, the Property Redress Scheme Ombudsman will make a binding decision that all parties must adhere to.

In short, your rent-to-rent business *must* join the PRS, according to the Consumers, Estate Agents, and Redress Act (CEARA) of 2007 (in England). Joining is easy and affordable. To join, you must submit an application which identifies the name of your business, the services you provide, the main point of contact, any additional branches of your business, and the personal details of at least one of your business partners. If you have no partners, it's you. When your application is accepted, you must pay an annual membership fee of £200 or less, depending on the type of membership you seek. When you've paid, the PRS provides a sticker for display at your place of operation, and leaflets which should be given to your clients; both property owners and tenants upon finalising and closing your contracts with each.

If you fail to join the PRS and a complaint is lodged against you, you risk having to submit and pay anyhow, and on top of that you risk fines. This is another step you just *do not* skip if you're operating

a respectable, ethical, and legitimate rent-to-rent
business. I know you agree that is the goal.

Gather Your Contracts

If your business is now set up, you're ready to start
gathering the contracts you'll need in order to
officially finalise the terms and conditions you've
established with your clients. At this point, we'll
assume you've chosen the sublet model that you're
going to start your business with. If you're ready to
start gathering contracts, you'll need to know if
you're using the AST model, the HMO model, or
the accommodations model. There are different
contracts for each of these models, and even
different subgroups of contracts under each of these
models depending on a variety of factors, such as
whether your property owner owns their property or
mortgages it.

You are going to need at least two major contracts
to get going: a management contract and a tenancy
contract. The management contract is formed
between you and the property owner, and the
tenancy contract is obviously formed between you
and the tenants you sublet to.

The good news is that once you've found template
contracts to use for both management and tenancy,
you can perform major and necessary edits to the
contract once, and you'll likely not need to make
these adjustments again for a while. Of course,
you'll always need to edit some specific details for

every single contract you draw up, but that's to be expected. The details of the terms and conditions will typically stay the same. That's not to say you can't edit the terms and conditions; that's up to you.

The better news is that despite the internet overflowing with property management and tenancy contracts, many trying to be sold, there's actually a wonderful organisation, that I have previously mentioned, that provides PDF versions of these contracts for free. Law Depot https://www.lawdepot.co.uk has been helping individuals and businesses with contracts since 2001, and they've served over 10 million parties in that time. Their library of contracts is extensive and covers not only the contracts you'll need for management and tenancy but anything you need for your business setup as well. They've got an in-house team of legal pros and an excellent, readily available staff to help you. They're easy to contact by phone, email, or even chat. They receive positive reviews and have been suggested as a trustworthy resource by businesses like The Wall Street Journal, Time Magazine, and The Washington Post.

GDPR Compliance

If you're not yet familiar with GDPR compliance, well, where have you been? Have you noticed that for the last year, every site you visit asks you to accept or refuse cookies? That's part of GDPR compliance. A minuscule part actually. GDPR or the General Data Protection Regulation is honestly an enormous concept with hundreds, if not thousands, of facets to it. GDPR deals with the protection, processing, storage, and movement of personal information collected through business and commerce.

If you stop for a moment and think about all of the various kinds of business and commerce that take place every day and all of the possible points in which any personal information is collected to do so, your head will start to swim. Personal information could be a name, a phone number or email address, an IP address, a credit card number; it can even be a business card you collected from someone at a networking event. There are seemingly endless points in a business interaction where personal information is collected. Once the information is collected, it's generally processed in some way and stored somehow, be it in a hardcopy file in your office, or in the digital cloud.

Since 2016, the European Commission has been

building the data protection regulation that would replace 1995's Data Protection Directive with clear and stringent rules for collecting, processing, storing, and moving personal data. In May 2018, GDPR compliance was rolled out and implemented, and any business found not complying is subject to hefty fines. Even though the UK plans to leave the European Union, it will still have to comply with GDPR ruling, and so will you. GDPR is easily the single most significant change in the way business is conducted in at least the last 25 years. It's no small concern, and you must be properly attentive to it.

The general idea behind GDPR is for businesses to increase the security and transparency of the personal information they collect. The EU does this by giving the owner of the personal data (the person whose data it is) more control over what happens with their information, and the ability to have that information removed from databases should they no longer wish for the business to possess it.

For you, that means any information you collect from prospects, property owners, tenants, suppliers, employees, or industry colleagues. So how is your rent-to-rent business supposed to handle all of this information in compliance with GDPR legislation? In the grand scheme, GDPR contains a complete eleven (long) chapters outlining all how a business should comply. While you may not need to understand all eleven chapters of this legislation at

this point, you should familiarise yourself with what
those chapters are in general. This way, as
situations arise, you know where to look to make
sure you're complying appropriately.

Everything GDPR can be found on the data
protection pages of the European Commission,
here: https://ec.europa.eu/info/law/law-topic/data-
protection_en. The site is remarkably well-
managed, current, and easy to use and search. The
information on the site comes directly from the
European Commission so you can be confident it's
accurate and up-to-date information. The eleven
chapters deal with the following:

General Provisions

This first section outlines the purposes and
definitions of general data protection. This section
will tell you that the "data owner" is the individual
to whom the data belongs; the person who can be
identified in any way at all by the information
collected. The "data controller" is the organisation
which collects the information. The "data
processor" is the organisation that processes the
information. The provisions section makes it clear
that GDPR compliance is strictly for business and
information you may collect personally, like the
phone number of a person you'd like to take on a
date, is not subject to GDPR compliance. This

section will give you a solid understanding of what GDPR is all about.

Principles

This section explains the moral and ethical implications of GDPR compliance; when it is and isn't permissible to collect, process, store, and move personal data. It covers factors about collecting personal information from individuals under legal age, and how long is legally appropriate to store data on individuals. Familiarising with the principles of GDPR is also a great idea because it gives your business an overall idea of the rights and wrongs of compliance, so again, when a situation arises, you have in the back of your mind that you should take a few minutes to investigate and make sure you're complying.

The Rights of the Data Owner

This section outlines and details the new level of control an individual has to dictate what an organisation does with the individual's personal information. For example, if I were to visit a site to download a management contract to use in my rent-to-rent business, the download is generally permitted only after I share my email address with the site. I can in theory, download that form, and then make a written request to the site to delete my personal information; my email address and that organisation must comply. They have a certain amount of time in which to remove my information from their databases, and any other associated database to which they've passed my information. Similarly, if an individual wants to know exactly what information an organisation holds on them, the organisation must comply and provide a complete profile of all the information they hold on that individual. At any time, an individual holds the right to have their information rectified or erased.

Controller and Processor

These sections breakdown and define everything that the controller and the processor must do with the information to comply with GDPR legislation. This includes how and when to process personal information, how to generate appropriate anonymity for parts of collected personal data. For example, when you enter your credit card number online and all numbers are X'ed out except for the last four digits, this is a version of Pseudonymisation, which is making part of the information unidentifiable for the protection of the individual. This is particularly important as we hear of more and more organisation sites getting hacked and personal information stolen. These sections explain how to officially process and store information and the security that goes along with it.

For example, if my business collects personal information from a tenant, I would store that information in a CRM database. But the supplier of that database and their servers must be GDPR-compliant servers, or it is I who violates compliance. It also includes several official resources an organisation may use to better learn about and comply with GDPR.

Liability and Penalties

This section defines the risks of non-compliance by any business organisation. This includes the warning process and the breakdown of fines your business faces should you be found to be non-compliant. It provides an understanding of what legal obligations the controller must adhere to and the consequences of not doing so.

B2B Marketing

GDPR draws a strict line between personal information collected for the purposes of business-to-consumer (B2C) marketing, such as a utility company storing information about its customers, and business-to-business (B2B) marketing, such as an accountant collecting information from the businesses it provides services to. If the world of rent-to-rent, you'll most likely be working in a B2C capacity, unless, for example, the property owner operates a business and it's that business you're actually interacting with when making agreements and contracts.

Restrictions

Final sections of the GDPR legislation cover unusual scenarios that deal with individual data protection. This includes compliance for situations like lawful interception of data, such as in the case of national security, military, police, and the justice system. It also includes collecting and storing of personal data for statistical and scientific purposes, deceased persons, and further restrictions for collecting and storing information on employees and partners.

While again, you probably don't need to be knee-deep in GDPR compliance as you begin your rent-to-rent business, there are a few steps your business should take from the outset to practice compliance. Get familiar with GDPR. Check! You've just done it. You now know where to find more information if you wish to become intimately familiar, as well.

Ensure three major components of GDPR compliance are evident on your business website. This includes making sure your site is secure, which means your website address should begin with "https" and not just "http". Your website should also implement the Cookie banner I mentioned earlier, which makes it obvious to any visitor of your site that your site uses cookies and it allows the visitor to accept or decline the use of cookies with their IP address. Finally, your site should update any opt-in form to comply with GDPR. For example, if you make a purchase online, often times one of the last checkboxes you see is the company asking if you'd like to receive marketing emails in the future from this company. This is compliant. What's not compliant is using the collected personal information to market to the individual in the future without having asked or notified the individual of such. The individual must always be presented with the ability to opt in- or - out of such practices.

With your familiarity and business site covered, the last step you should take is to ensure your suppliers are also compliant. For example, if you use Salesforce.com to store your CRM information, you should make sure that Salesforce.com is also compliant (they are) or your business is in violation, for the pure fact that it's your own responsibility to choose your suppliers carefully.

For every tool, freelancer, or B2B business you work with, you should make sure they comply. Because GDPR is such a big issue, most suppliers provide a page on their own site that explains their level of GDPR compliance. If you scroll to the bottom of

most any site, you'll find links to items such as
Terms and Conditions, Privacy Policy, and Cookies
Preferences. If you visit these pages, you'll find the
information you need. If you're unable to find this
information, you can request this information from
your supplier, and in theory, your request should be
provided in a matter of days. If your supplier is
unwilling or hesitant to share this information, your
safest bet is to find an alternative supplier for that
particular service.

Set up your Professional Image and Status

You've done it! If you've made it this far and come through the heavy details of beginning your business, here's a reward for you. This is the step in which you set up aspects of your business that really start to make it take shape and dimension and make it feel real. With your business structure, licence, insurance, and PRS membership out of the way, it's time to bring your business to life. Here are six strides to take that will feel really good.

Business Banking

If you've chosen to operate as a sole trader, setting up a business banking account is advised but not mandatory. On the other hand, if you've chosen to operate as a limited company or a partnership, a business banking account is required. Here again, is a small lesson to learn from my own mistakes.

Operating as a sole trader out of your own personal banking account might feel nice when the money goes in, but the good feeling pretty much ends there. Keeping track of your business finances through your own banking account is a mess and a headache for you, and especially for your accountants and bookkeepers. Operating out of your own personal banking account is also restrictive and

perhaps even a violation according to your
bank. When you operate a business from a personal
bank account, banks aren't too fond. There's
probably a stipulation in your bank's terms and
conditions which states that your personal banking
account is for *personal* use only. Further, a personal
banking account won't cut it if you want to apply for
business loans or take credit card payments from
your clients.

My advice: just get the business banking
account. The cost is very minimal and the setup
protects you better and often comes with a variety of
business banking solutions that will make your life
easier and your business grow faster. Your business
income and expenses will quickly become a hassle to
track, especially if you're managing multiple
properties and tenants. This is going to cause
serious complications when the time comes to
submit accurate tax returns.

Bookkeeping

Okay, maybe not the most enjoyable reward, but it
does bring life to your operation to start getting
numbers on the books. But how? This relatively
complicated process is made super-simple with
software. QuickBooks (https://quickbooks.com) is
the most popular solution for small
businesses. QuickBooks even offers additional

features and support for those working in the sublet vertical, so it's basically a perfect place to start. In previous years, QuickBooks was a piece of software that required your purchase and download, but as the cloud has become more versatile and reliable, so too has QuickBooks. It's now available online and without download so that you can access it from any browser and device. An account only takes about 5 minutes to set up and link with your bank.

QuickBooks makes it simple to manage your business' income and expenses, invoices, taxes, reporting and analytics, receipts, 1099s, bills, and projected profitability. Perhaps the best news is that within your account, user permissions can be granted. This is excellent functionality if you want to share access to this account with partners or accountants and bookkeepers, especially if you want to protect sensitive information. QuickBooks can even help you find a bookkeeper to manage this for you if it's in your budget. There are many packages from which to select starting under £20/month for a basic start and ranging to about £100/month for advanced options, such as a complete payroll automation package. The cost of QuickBooks is tax-deductible for your business and free phone, email, and chat support is included in your free trial and purchase.

Even if QuickBooks doesn't sound like the right option for you, there are alternative software

applications to select from. My personal advice,
however, is that QuickBooks is the most trusted,
most widely used, and provides the most
functionality for the fairest cost, so it's a no-brainer.

Contact Information

Now that you're official it's time to look official and
this is a lot more fun than bookkeeping. Get
yourself a business phone number and a business
email address. Both are pretty simple to secure, you
just need to make a few choices about how you want
this to go. Often times, a rent-to-rent business
professional just starting out will use a personal cell
phone number and email address. There's nothing
wrong with this as a sole trader, but if you're
operating as a limited company or partnership,
you're going to need official contact information
anyway. One thing to think about if you're going to
start with the email and phone number you already
have, is that now the public essentially has access to
your personal number and email address and this can
soon become rather annoying, especially if you like
to keep your personal life separate from your
business life.

Another detail to consider if you're using your own
email address is professionalism. You don't want to
be dispensing an email address that looks
unprofessional, overly-revealing, or offensive. This

is very easily avoided and free to overcome. Create a free and separate email address for your business communications with Gmail, or any other number of email client services. It used to be thought that an address ending with "@gmail.com" looked unprofessional but that belief has in large part disappeared, and you'll find many professionals now use Gmail and the like for their business email. Email from your business account can even be forwarded to your personal account and filtered appropriately so you don't have to check multiple accounts throughout your day.

A third option, and my personal favourite is that when you acquire a website domain and host, you often get a free email account (or multiple) that matches your site. This is the most professional image. Your email will look something like: John@website.com, where the "website" will be your domain name and will match your site and business name.

Business phone numbers work in much the same way. Your phone provider can often offer you a secondary number at a lower cost and bundle it into your monthly bill. The phone number can be forwarded to your cell or another phone line and you'll be able to easily determine if someone is calling you for personal interaction or business interaction by which number they called, even if it all goes to the same line. It's essentially like using an alias phone number. If you're really lucky, sometimes a website even comes with a phone number, though these offers are more costly and harder to find.

Answering Services

At first, it might sound like an answering service is an unnecessary expense, but as you become busier with work, it will sound like a godsend. The truth is that most of these services are actually very affordable and can be as low as £25/month. If your rent-to-rent business is a side business at this point, an answering service makes even more sense. If prospects and clients call while you're at your other job, someone is still there to answer and direct the call or take the message professionally. Answering services offer a host of features, but you'll want to look for one that offers a reasonable price, a live receptionist (24/7 is even better), tailored care, ease-of-use, and excellent customer support. One of the best I've had the pleasure of using previously was (https://www.takemycalls.co.uk/) which offers an enormous amount of service and features for a very low and reasonable rate. As you grow, these services can scale with you to support your growing needs.

Regardless of the business structure you operate under, an answering service is not a mandatory requirement, but it sure does help your professional image. If TakeMyCalls doesn't look right for you, search for some of their competitors and see if you can find an offer that works perfectly for you as you're starting out. Remember that you can always start with a basic package to try it out and increase features and services as needed. When prospects and clients call for information and help, they may not get the answer they need at that moment, but hearing someone on the other end of the phone, as opposed to a voicemail message, instils a greater deal of confidence in you and your business and it cultivates a feeling of being taken care of at the moment. Many of these services even integrate with other applications like your CRM, so that each call is recorded and listed under the proper contact, so you'll always be able to reference who called, when, and why from your CRM database, and you can track whether the call request has been resolved or still needs your attention.

Online Presence

Though it is not mandatory for any business type, you'll soon find it's pretty difficult to market your business without some form of an online presence. Most often, this is a website, but it can be something a simple as a Facebook or LinkedIn account for your business. A dedicated website certainly looks most professional, but that's not to say you can't sculpt your social media to look highly professional as well. Truly, the key is professionalism.

Creating a professional business site is easy if you know-how and have the time, but if you don't, you can again turn to freelance sites like Fiverr to find a professional that can build this for you. If you need to do this yourself for budgetary reasons, there's still a wealth of tools to help. You'll be responsible for purchasing a domain and finding a host. In most cases, the vendor from which you purchase your domain (such as GoDaddy.com) also offers hosting services. Your website domain can be as little as £5 annually, and hosting services usually cost around £10-20/month. The cost of your domain will largely depend on the keywords you want to use and the suffix you select. Words that are more popular and have a greater demand are going to cost more. A suffix like ".com", as opposed to ".biz" is also going to cost a bit more. This is where it takes a little bit of creativity to come up with a website name that's not already taken, and not unreasonably expensive. The possible combinations are infinite, and with a little focus, you'll find something that fits you perfectly. Avoid creating a domain that's hard to read, type, spell or has numbers or symbols in it. These cause undue hassle in the marketing process. If you don't have a domain, you don't need a host and if you don't get a host, there's no reason to buy a domain. This is one reason vendors offer them together.

Creating an entire website when you don't have all that much to say yet can be a big project. You'll want to incorporate a fair amount of web content and imagery that supports your business, such as images of your properties. Writing the content and adding the pictures can be time-consuming. This is another good reason to seek out a freelancer for help. However, there's another popular option. You can create a web presence for your business with one landing page rather than an entire site. You'll still need to acquire a domain and hosting, but there will be a lot less to set up and manage, and a landing page can still display and capture everything you need to get the job done. Selecting a landing page can be a perfect start to your business and then in the future, once you've grown in experience and size, you can switch to a full site if necessary.

If you choose to create a presence for your business using a social media platform (or several), this cuts the cost significantly. You won't need to acquire a domain or hosting, but keep in mind you won't have as much freedom naming your profile link or suffix. Still, your presence can look mighty professional, and again, if you don't have time to do this setup yourself, a freelancer can help you for a nominal fee. With a social media platform, you also don't need to worry so much about GDPR compliance because when an individual visits a platform like

Facebook, LinkedIn, YouTube, or Instagram, consent is implied. However, if you employ or link to business forms from the social media site, you'll still need to make sure to include the proper opt-out options on your forms.

Whichever option you go with, having an online presence in today's world is almost a necessity, especially if you plan to market online. Further, a web presence builds a rapport and sense of ease and trust with your prospects and clients. Pick something that fits your budget to start and bring your business to life online.

Business Cards

Last but not least, get some business cards made up so you can hand them to prospects, clients, and colleagues when networking and conducting business. Providing a business card will make a great impression and make it very easy for your clients and prospects to get in touch with you. Your card should be professional yet eye-catching and memorable. There are plenty of custom card creation tools and printing options available online, but one of the easiest and least expensive options is Vistaprint (https://www.vistaprint.com). This site allows you to customise the look of your card, front and back, and set the number of cards you want to be printed. Better yet, Vistaprint is almost always offering discounts and deals. A pack of 500 cards can often cost you as little as £10-20 depending on the customisation and number of cards.

If actual cards aren't really your preference, the world of technology has you covered with digital business cards. You can design a business card online that can be given digitally to your clients and prospects. There are benefits to this route, as well. Mainly, the card rarely is lost since it's in the cloud. Plus, no printing means your operation is that much eco-friendlier. Still, it can take a little getting used to, for you to give and for others to receive. Transferring your digital business card from your phone to a prospect's phone at a networking event sounds good, but you don't want to be fumbling with your phone, or making them fumble with yours. Sometimes the old way is still the best and handing someone a traditional business card can be the simplest and most professional option.

You're only half-way done, and you've accomplished so much already! At this point, your rent-to-rent business is fully set up and operational — time to get to work.

Chapter 4:

5-Step Process to Find Rental Properties

Your business is registered, insured, and you've joined the redress scheme. Your 12-month business plan is written, and your contracts are gathered. Your sublet model is selected. You have a strong understanding of the rules and regulations you must follow. Your business presence is established. Time to put everything in motion, find some properties in some lucrative locations, and make some money.

In this section, I'll go over the five steps you will take every time you search for new properties to sublet. Over the next year, you will repeat these steps and learn their nuances. This will allow you to refine your process. By refining your process, you will continuously find properties that are more and more attractive, in better and better locations. By polishing these steps, your process becomes sharper, cuts faster, and slices a larger piece of the pie.

Step 1: Location, Location, Location

Even if you've never heard of subletting until now, you know the expression. What are the three most important factors in real estate? Location.

The first step is to find three lucrative areas that are nearby enough for you to reach easily. Go out far enough that you're reaching profitable zones, but not so far that they're inconvenient.

You're looking for locations that offer a higher rental cost. Aim for locations that are already affluent, unless one of your missions is to better communities through property management. Don't get too selective. It's a bit like shopping in the market. You want a high-quality brand, but maybe not the highest quality. For a beginner, aim for a location you would rate 4 or 5 stars; a place you might even like to live.

I'll point out now, it can be a smart idea to search for locations you might rate 3 stars. These places have often got a lot of room for improvement, and your preparation and early expertise will work for you here. These places are also often targets of tenants because the cost is lower, but the location and properties are still something they can work with and see their families in. This gives you the opportunity to work your negotiation skills and strike a bargain with property owners for a lower guaranteed rent, but a professional and well-managed property. When they get a load of your preparedness and expertise, the offer will very likely look appealing to them. Be careful, and make sure your property owners are on the up and up as well as you.

Start with about 10 locations you're pretty sure would offer a handsome profit. Then begin knocking down one after the other until you have the three best locations left. You will filter your 10 locations out by studying a few key factors for each of them. Over time, and depending on your general location, you'll be able to find which factors are really the best for determining prime location. To start off, investigate the following for each location:

- Average annual household income
- Average cost of buying a home
- Average mortgage rates
- Average rental cost
- Tax history
- Average tenant turnover rates
- Rise in home values
- Rise in rental values
- Job availability
- Unemployment rates
- Nearby school systems and ratings
- Nearby universities and ratings
- Public transportation

- Public resources
- Crime rates
- Utilities access and average costs

One by one, decide if the location is good enough for you. Put it on the keep list or in the bin until you're left with your three perfect starting locations.

Step 2: Find Viable Properties

You're looking for properties that will match your budget and bandwidth, but still deliver a handsome monthly profit in any of the three locations you've decided upon.

Find your properties with three basic tactics. Dig through local listings, market your business to these three locations, and network in these areas.

Dig

The internet is an endless resource, but visit these locations and pick up local printed listings as well. Use both as it's often the case that the best properties are listed in one but not the other. Think of how you would find an apartment if you were a tenant, find some that have come available (or will), and then find out who owns them and contact those people with your offer.

Market

Whatever you've decided your marketing plan to be, apply it to these three areas. Consider direct mail marketing to related businesses and property owners and customise the marketing to fit the correct audience. Consider running Google Ads or Facebook Ads for your offer in these three locations. Look for landlord listings online and send them

directly or email marketing for your offer. It's a
numbers game; the more people exposed to your
offer, the more that will take it.

Network

Take time to network online and in real life, in
these locations. Online, again, the possibilities
never end. Use your business LinkedIn profile and
network the hell out of it. LinkedIn is the
Facebook of the professional world. The platform is
built on the idea of growing your network
quickly. You really can't afford to not use it.

Similarly, Facebook is loaded with groups you can
join for networking in the industry and related
industries, and in the exact locations you're
targeting. I repeat, "related industries". Don't stop
your network at real estate and property
management; think of everyone these individuals
interact with on a professional level. A local cleaning
service or repairman might be your link to the
perfect landlord and the perfect property. Network
in real life. Find related networking events in the
three locations you're targeting and attend them.
Go prepared with your business card and perhaps a
one-page piece of marketing to quickly illustrate
your amazing offer. This could even be a version of
your direct mail marketing.

Step 3: Investigate Relevant Local Codes and Regulations

You already know what you're responsible for in terms of overall legal regulations for your business and operations, but there could be a different game afoot in your chosen locations. Do a bit of homework on the local laws, codes, and regulations as they relate to subletting. If there are other rules to be aware of and adhere to, build these into your 12-month plan when you land a property there.

Step 4: Size Up Local Competition

While you're sizing things up, don't forget the local competition. Who else in these three areas is making an offer like yours? How long have they been operating? What does their online presence look like? Which properties do they maintain? Are there reviews of the competition? Do a mini SWOT analysis, but on them. Get to know them at networking events. Sometimes the competition can become your best friend.

Step 5: Run the Numbers

As prospects begin to line up, get a sense for the financial aspects you're working with and start to run some numbers. Outline what you think a great offer would be for guaranteed rent and the property management service you'll offer to supplement it. Outline what you think a competitive but enticing offer will be for your subletters. Outline a projected income to cost estimate. Consider your payback periods on anything you've used to start your business. Generate for yourself a cheat sheet of these points so that when you actually throw out the bait to your prospect, you have an aim.

That's it. Five steps and you're ready to make an offer to your property owners and subletters. These are the five steps that, over the course of your first year, you will become very familiar with through constant repetition each time you go out for more property. This repetition will cause you to sharpen your skills in these areas and the process will start to go faster and more efficiently. Remember, if you can - delegate. Paying a virtual assistant to gather, organise, and filter any of the information in these steps in a way that will speed up the ultimate decision-making process for you, is worth the cost. Especially with your healthy growing profit.

Chapter 5:

Your Viewing and Signing Process

Now that you've found a few properties in your
three initial locations, it's time to check them out
and negotiate a deal with the property
owners. Once your agreements have been made
with your property owners or landlords, it's time to
get prospective tenants through the doors to view
each unit and find the perfect match between
landlord - you - tenant - and the unit and location
itself. In this section, we'll take a look at the steps
you will take to negotiate with your landlords and

property owners. Then, I'll walk you through the details of viewing your units with prospective tenants, screening those tenants, and signing a rental agreement with them. With these steps done, you're ready to start collecting rent and managing your properties.

Viewing and Negotiations with Property Owners

Let's assume you've contacted a handful of property owners with your initial offer of managing their property and tenancies and they've taken the bait. You've been in communication with the property owners and it's time for you to view the properties and strike a deal. Now I'll walk you through exactly what you should be thinking and doing to make sure this interaction goes smoothly and professionally with each of your property owners.

Prepare for the Interaction

First things first. Preparation. Nothing can make a prospective property owner more sceptical of your offer than making it up on the spot. Of course there are almost always unforeseen changes and considerations that will affect your final offer and contract, but if you don't walk in with some sort of benchmark on what you're looking to do in profit and management in general, you'll almost certainly end up with a heap of management work and expenses but a rental that will leave you still struggling for profit. Set yourself for success before you meet with the property owner by bringing with you the numbers you've started to run on other units in the area - and don't just bring them - keep the key points in mind as you view the property and discuss possibilities with your prospective owner. Your key points are going to be:

- How long is the term of rental for you?
- What needs to be done to the property to rent it out?
- What is the cost of guaranteed rent you're expecting?
- Does the owner own outright, or are they mortgaging the property?
- Is the property properly insured?
- What has been the average cost to rent this unit in the past for tenants?
- Is there additional management, utilities, security issues you need to act on?

The idea is to get a good sense of what it will take to rent the property, what level of work will be involved to make the unit ready and then manage it going forward, and of course, what kind of profit will you be making after these management costs have been covered.

It's also a smart idea to bring a copy of your business plan, for your reference, but perhaps also for the prospective owner to skim through if they should have in-depth questions. Typically, they will not have in-depth questions at this point. When you hand them your contractual offer for signing, that's when the questions will come, but it's always better to be prepared; not to mention it conveys a much more professional and experienced image to come with these details in hand. At this point, your prospective owners want to know that your operation is legitimate and that you're not going to cause them a loss or undue stress and management themselves. They may want to know why your offer is better than hiring an agency to rent out the property. You know the answer to this is your sweet-as-honey deal which includes guaranteed rent, zero-gap loss, and responsible management. These are not offers a typical agency will make. The agency helps to fill the unit with properly screened tenants, and that's about where the agency offer ends.

Your figures are prepared and in mind; what else needs your preparation before you meet with the prospective property owner? Yourself. Don't show up in street clothes. It seems like it goes without saying, but it happens often and kills the deal before it began. This is the time when your personal appearance will work for you or against you, so dress appropriately and communicate deliberately, both in terms of body language and verbal language. Your appearance should be professional but approachable. You don't necessarily need to throw on the executive 3-piece suit, but if you'd wear it to the gym or lounging around your home, it's out. Go with clean, crisp, business casual. Are you arriving by car? Consider cleaning out your vehicle and sending it through a wash before you show up. These are the small and significant details that help others to form an opinion about you, so don't neglect them.

Viewing the Property

In some cases, you may be viewing a property that is currently occupied by a tenant. Be respectful. Find out if any current tenants will be continuing their rentals, or if they will be leaving soon.

While viewing the property with the property owner, you'll want to view every single space in the unit that you'll be responsible for managing. This includes the sometimes overlooked utilities closest, the attic, the basement, security systems, and the yard and the perimeter of the property. Get an idea of how and when waste and rubbish are removed and the cost of doing so. Find out if the previous tenants have had pets and children if possible. This can also help you gauge any repairs or fixes that might be needed before showing the property to prospective tenants. Does the owner currently (or have they in the past) hire landscapers to take care of the outside of the property, will this responsibility now fall upon you and your property management, and what's the general expense of this upkeep?

Inside the unit, be sure to check every room and pay

additional attention to the kitchen and bathroom, as
these are almost always where you find expensive
repairs that may be needed before you're able to rent
the unit again. While assessing needed repairs,
consider larger alterations that might be necessary to
turn a traditional AST property into an HMO, for
example. Note windows, doors, and locks. Will any
need replacing to make the property safe and secure
again? Door locks almost always need replacing for
the safety and security of your next tenants. Ask
your property manager to show you how heating,
gas, and electric works for the unit, and get a feel for
whether you'll be taking on these utilities or if the
owner plans to keep them in his or her own
name. Typically, the owner can't wait to get rid of
extra bills, so it sweetens the deal for them if you're
willing to transfer the utilities to yourself or the
next tenant.

As you go through the property, you'll be keeping in
mind expenses as you go, but take notes. The mind
will inevitably forget or mix up details, especially if
you're viewing multiple properties with multiple
managers. Write your notes down as you're viewing.
When you get back to the office to draw up an
official contract, these notes are invaluable. One
detail you forgot to note can set your whole plan
akimbo and skew the profit you were set on.

Assess Your Timeframe

The length of time in which you have to work, to fill the unit, is key. You'll need to consider when current tenants will be out if the unit is occupied. You'll need to determine how long you have once they are gone to make repairs and alterations if any are necessary. Map out how long those fixes will take and what you'll be responsible for paying for during that time. Once those changes are made, you'll need time to show and sign the unit. Consider all of these aspects on your timeframe so you know roughly when you're looking to start making a profit. The bottom line is: how long until you can collect your first payment from your new tenant?

Questions and Insights

Don't be fearful of asking questions. A legitimate owner is going to be happy to share whatever information they can to get a trustworthy manager and a guaranteed rent. The more relevant questions you ask about the history of the unit, the better it is for both of you. Not only does this demonstrate what a conscientious professional you are, but often details will come from these questions that can help you to bargain for a better contract with them. For example, if you need to perform repairs that will equal a significant amount, you may be able to bargain for a lower guaranteed rent in your first year, and this leaves room for the owner to raise it reasonably for you in the second year.

As long as you keep the questions reasonable (don't get overly personal), you really can't ask too many questions. As you move through the property and talk with the owner, questions will come to you. Ask them as they come and take notes. At the start of this process, you may be nervous about whether you're asking the right questions. Remember that you're prepared and educated on the topic; you're asking the right questions if it's giving you insight. As you practice this process over the next year, you'll get the hang of what to ask and what you can leave out. Keep in mind that sometimes the significance of a question can change from location to location, from unit to unit, and from sublet model to sublet model.

The Contract and the Close

In some cases, though typically rarer, you may be able to go for the close on the spot. However, this means you've come with a contract for each of you to sign, and you're confident the owner wants to make a decision today. In a case such as this, more than likely, you've done the majority of your question-asking and profit-and-expense-figuring before you even get to the unit. You've already drawn up the contract for signing. However, it's a tricky job to write up a final contract without knowing the deal with the property so my advice, at least to start, is: don't count on signing today. Instead, gather every last shred of information you need and then inform the owner you'll be sending a contract for consideration and signing within the next 24 hours.

Back at the office, take the time to consider all of your notes, all of the other properties you're aiming for or already managing, your timeframe, and your expenses. With time to consider these and plot out your expected income and costs, you can confidently draw up a contract that will suit you and the owner, and make the deal a no-brainer for them. Send the offer via email within the 24-hour period you indicated, and then allow your owner another 24 hours to review this offer. It may seem like a fast process, but you also don't want to give your owner enough time to reconsider or drag their heels. After

the 24 hours you've allocated for the owner to
review the offer, call them. This is your closing call.

A word of warning here: no matter how enthusiastic
your in-person meeting is, you cannot count on this
alone. Often, property owners (or people in general)
want to naturally convey a friendly and positive
attitude in such an interaction. Individuals tend to
avoid confrontation, so a sunny disposition upfront
doesn't always mean your owner carries that through
the next 48 hours. Expect that when the owner is
alone with time to review the offer, that questions
and concerns of their own will pop up and you need
to be at the ready to stanch them. If the enthusiasm
has dwindled, the closing call is your chance to
rejuvenate it.

As you go into your call, your number one goal is
this: do not sell your offer. Sell their solution. The
property owner is interested in your offer because it
solves a number of their own problems. Use this
call to remind them (directly and indirectly) of these
problems and your solutions for them. Focus on
them, not you, and not your deal. You're always
pitching the solution to these problems, not your
contract. When concerns and objections arise, do
not try to skip over them; address them. Suggest a
way that these concerns would be alleviated through
your management. Illustrate how these concerns are
covered in your solutions. If you sense hesitation,

ask the prospect to share their thoughts with you. "Tell me your thoughts" is a powerful phrase to demonstrate caring, but more so for you to read your prospect and what's holding them back from signing.

As you speak with your prospective owner on your closing call, do more listening than talking. Much will be revealed to you about any apprehensions at this moment. Don't get trigger-happy; don't get trigger-shy. Utilise the following closing tactics with calm and steady determination, and you'll hit the mark.

Yes or No

Avoid asking questions that result in a yes/no answer. This is a trick I learned going way back to cold-calling and appointment-setting days. Here's an example: "Do you want to meet with our rep to find out how he can save you money?" That's going to be a "yes" or a "no", and guess which one it probably is. After a hefty number of "no"s, I learned to adjust my phrasing. "Do you want to meet with our rep Tuesday or Friday?" Now you've given the prospect a choice, but both choices will equal a "yes". The hefty collection of "no" soon became a hefty collection of "yes". Don't feel bad about it, either. It's often the case that the prospect does actually want your help, but they've been preconditioned to suss out scams and protect themselves. It's going to take your clever phrasing and communication to break through those protective barriers discreetly, to truly help them.

Problem Solver

Reiterate, directly or subtly, the problems and challenges you know your prospect faces, and how your offer solves these. If the problem that causes hesitation is X, demonstrate how your offer covers X with a solution, or how you can work that into the plan. Eliminate X in their mind. To draw out these concerns and set them clear as solved in the prospect's mind, try getting them to say your solution. Try to draw this out with phrases like:

- "Is there any reason why not?"
- "If you were to do this, how will it help you?"
- "If I can find a way to address X, would you sign the agreement by [tomorrow]?"
- "In your opinion, does this solve all of your problems?"

Use Help

"Help" is a magic word. Whether you're offering it or asking for it, the word "help" can take the individual from off the defensive and protective track of mind, and reposition them to a more humanistic and empathetic track of mind. "Would you like my help?" is a fantastic question, because whether they say it or not, they do want help. They are waiting for someone to come along and solve their problems. The idea that a problem-solver is right in front of them (literally or figuratively) is very tempting. The prospect considers how wonderful it would feel to get the thing they want: a problem solver. They do want your help or you would not have made it this far with this prospect.

"Can I help you?" is great, but you know what's even more powerful? "I need your help." Convey that the plan you've laid out is all the help they need, but you need a bit of help from them. Accentuate that you need a small piece of help from them to get this wonderful plan underway, and that help is to approve the agreement with their signature.

Here Today, Gone Tomorrow

One of your best friends in negotiations and closing is the scarce deal. Introduce scarcity to help nudge your prospect along. Whether you're selling widgets or a 5-star property management package, knowing that the deal is fleeting will set fire under your prospect. Here's the opportunity, don't let it pass you by. There are several ways to convey this, but here are a few key phrases to try out:

- "This opportunity is going to help some property owner in [location], I don't see why it shouldn't be you"
- "I'd hate to see you stay stuck where you are...let's take the step now to prevent that."
- "I know you want a solution in place by [date] so with that in mind, perhaps we should move to the final agreement and get the ball rolling."

If, Then

The If/Then setup is often used to drive the point home toward the end of the conversation. It's a tool to remind the prospect again, if you continue down the same path, then you get the same results. That's assuming the results have been less than desirable, like a vacant unit. You can set the phrasing up to be something like: "If you pass on this deal, then you can expect more of what you've had; a vacant unit; an unmanaged unit; rent without guarantee". Don't be too harsh, but don't be afraid of being direct.

Let It Go

If you've pulled out all the stops and you still get hesitation and delay, don't obsess on it; move on. It's not the right deal for you, and that delay could be a sign of worse struggles to come with that property owner. It's not worth your precious time. You know your offer is excellent so take it to someone else who recognises its worth.

Viewing and Negotiations with Tenants

Let's assume you've signed with your property owner and it's time to start showing your unit to prospective tenants. There are two major ways this can go: showing a unit while it's still occupied, or when it's vacant. Showing a unit when it's vacant is a much more desirable scenario, but we work with what we have.

There are benefits to both, though my personal opinion is that despite its minor disadvantages, showing a vacant space is better. If the accommodation is still occupied when you show it, at least the likelihood of a tenancy gap and rent loss is lessened. Another minor benefit is that your utility transfer will only be from the last tenant to the next, and you'll not need to be the middleman on that. This is, however, null if you plan to keep the utilities in your name and add that into the cost of the unit for the next tenant. On the other hand, if you have to show the accommodation when there's a tenant still occupying it, there's no real guarantee it will be clean and presentable. Further, the tenant may not be co-operative and could try to sabotage the viewing. Worse still, the tenant may be late in leaving, which will compromise the date your new tenant is supposed to move in. One tactic I've found that works well in these scenarios is a friendly little incentive. Consider how far it can go when you offer a gift card to the current tenant, for a nice restaurant or a local shop to furnish the new space that the old tenant will be moving to. A £25-50 gift card can make your transition smooth and easy. Keep in mind though that another drawback that comes with an immediate transfer from old tenant to new is the lack of time in between tenancies where you're able to get in there to clean and make repairs and changes. This, specifically, will be an aspect of the sublet you need to keep in mind and work out with your new tenant.

If you are working with a tenant that currently occupies the space, be respectful to their space. Communicate clearly and well ahead of time when you plan to show the unit. Ask the current tenant to pick up the accommodation and secure any animals that might be in the unit. If there's a tenant occupying the space, it's a bad idea to post "For Rent" signs outside the apartment. This inevitably leads to random individuals walking up to the unit as asking the current tenant about renting and viewing the apartment. Not only is this a hassle for the current tenant, but it spoils your hard work. You don't know what that tenant will say to your prospect or if they'll even be friendly. Don't leave this to chance. Place your ads in print and online and direct interested parties to contact you directly via phone or email. This way, a viewing time can be set that works for all parties involved.

If the unit is vacant, you risk losing money on rent
and you'll likely have to pay for the utilities to stay
on between tenancies, but the benefits are worth it,
in my opinion. Vacant accommodation gives you
the opportunity to get in there and make
appropriate repairs and to clean the accommodation.
This can often include minor fixes and painting, rug
cleaning, tile replacement, cabinet door replacement,
and so forth. This can be quite a bit harder to
manage if your new tenant has already moved in.

With a vacant space, you have the opportunity to
not only clean, but stage the accommodation so that
it's warm, cosy, and inviting. The right staging can
help prospective tenants to imagine themselves in
the unit living happily with furnishings and
accoutrements they want to live with and
enjoy. Not only can you control the look and feel of
the accommodation, but you can control how the
accommodation smells and how warm and inviting
it is when prospective tenants enter. Another benefit
to working with vacant accommodation is that
scheduling is quite a bit easier. This may translate
to a gap in the tenancy for a brief time, but trying to
schedule a time to show the unit that works for all
parties can end up causing significant delay.

Now let's assume that whether the accommodation
is vacant or not, you have prospective tenants lined

up to see it. What do you need to do?

Legally, you need to show each and every space/room that the tenant will have access to, including storage, basement, attic, garden, everything. If they can go into the space in their tenancy, you need to show that space during the viewing.

What's more, steering a prospect is bad form and it can just as easily set you up for liability. Steering is trying to show off a certain part of the accommodation whilst skipping over other parts that are perhaps not as attractive or convenient. However, doing this can actually be construed as discrimination. For example, if a prospective tenant comes to see the accommodation and that individual is disabled in some way, and you avoid showing the individual a part of the unit, it could be seen as a liability for which you can suffer consequences before you've even begun to rent. Avoid this by showing every prospective tenant every inch of space they will have access to.

Prepare for Questions from the Tenant

Do you remember the list of important aspects you used to find your location and the property? Your prospective tenants will have the same concerns so you should have as much of that information at the ready as possible. Anticipate the questions your tenants will bring to you, and beat them to the punch. If you can, demonstrate the answer during the showing. If the question happens to be about a security gate, show the prospective tenant what they need to know about the security for the accommodation. If you cannot demonstrate, have facts handy. A tenant may ask you about local school systems or public transportation. Prepare by gathering these details before you meet so that your prospective tenant gets the information they need, and you look like a professional.

Know the Area

It's not just the property that tenants want to know about. Especially if they're moving a significant distance from their last residence, prospective tenants want to know about the great location you're working in and what it has to offer. Prepare your notes or do a little internet research before you meet with tenants and prepare for questions like:

- What are the schools like in the area?
- Is there public transportation?
- Are there any local parks?
- Are there any local gyms?
- What's the crime rate like? Burglaries?
- Are there any noise nuisances? High traffic? Nightclubs?

- Is the area prone to flooding and other natural disasters?
- What are the neighbours like?

Exterior Property

The exterior of the property is the first thing prospects will see so if you can, clean up and repair this area as well and stage it. It doesn't have to be much. Depending on the exterior, you may need to make fence or gate repairs, mailbox repairs, garden and lawn maintenance and anything else that draws the eye in a negative way. Better yet- anything with the potential to draw the eye in a positive way should be the things you focus on. Showing the exterior will give you an opportunity to answer questions like:

- Who is responsible for garden maintenance?
- Is there an extra cost for it?
- Is it shared?
- Are tenants allowed to garden?
- Should tenants expect any upcoming exterior repairs or changes?
- How is the exterior of the unit secured? Gates? Door and window locks? Security and alarm systems? Floodlights?
- Has the unit ever had a break-in?

Interior Property

The inside of the property is where tenants typically have the most questions and concerns. If you've had the opportunity to repair and clean the unit and stage it, you could very well head off these questions simply by appearances. Still, be ready to address some of the more pressing concerns that typically come up. Prepare to answer questions like:

- Are there any signs of dampness or mould?
- Are any repairs still required?
- Are tenants allowed to paint the walls?
- Does the unit come furnished in any way? Does it come with basic appliances?
- Is there central heating? Do the radiators all work? Where are they throughout the home?
- How's the water pressure and hot water? Are there any leaky pipes or dripping taps? Do sinks and showers drain well?
- Is the accommodation insulated? Are there any draughts?
- Is there storage space? Is it shared?
- Can tenants put up shelving, decor, and curtains?

Security, Safety, and Utilities

When you take over accommodation, the safety and security regulations are a very significant responsibility for you. All relevant regulations must be met and sometimes this means replacing old fire alarms and making sure fire exits are easily accessible. If the accommodation is to be rented as an HMO, there are some additional security and safety issues you may need to address. For example, fire alarms, extinguishers, and blankets must be available in the accommodation for emergencies. Take time to go through these aspects of the property as you show it to prospective tenants. Be prepared to answer questions like:

- Does the accommodation include fire alarms? How many? Have they been tested?
- Are there fire extinguishers in the accommodation? How many?
- Are there fire blankets in the kitchen and elsewhere?
- Are fire regulations adhered to and addressed?
- Are there carbon monoxide detectors in the accommodation?
- Where are the fire exits and how accessible are they?
- Have you got a current Landlords gas certificate?
- Have you undertaken a Legionnaires' disease risk assessment?
- Are there any electrical wiring or outlet concerns? How many outlets are there throughout the unit?

- Are there working telephone and cable points in the unit?
- How's the Wi-Fi signal?
- How does waste removal work?

The Agreement and the Costs

The prospective tenant will undoubtedly have questions of their own, but this is a good opportunity for you to ask questions of the tenant. Questions will go both ways and this is a great way for you to pre-screen tenants for whether or not they'll be a good match for the unit and your management. Focus on setting proper expectations up front to gauge how well your prospect accepts them. Share and collect information on the following points:

- How much is the rent each month?
- Is a first, last, and secure payment required? How much are they?
- Are pets allowed? Is there an additional cost for pets?
- Are utilities included in the cost or are they separate? Is the tenant responsible for them? What are the average utility costs for the unit?
- Are there additional costs to the accommodation the tenant is responsible for?
- Is there a late fee for rent paid late?

- Is there a tenancy agreement that can be shared for review?

Finding Tenants and Conducting Viewings

You now have a solid understanding of many of the questions and aspects that will come up as you show the accommodation to prospective tenants, but let's take a moment to go over a well-organised and deliberate showing. First of all, you need to find some potential tenants. Obviously using agents to list a property or bedroom incurs a fee, which will eat into your profits. If listing the whole property, you can use Facebook Marketplace, Facebook groups in the local area or Gumtree to advertise. If you are using the HMO model, I advise you to do all of the above, in addition to listing each room on www.spareroom.com and other similar websites. These websites are responsible for filling 90% of my vacant rooms, and the turnaround time is incredible. So many young professionals or students are looking for an affordable room because renting a one-bedroom property could cost them three times the amount. For every accommodation you show to someone, you should have a basic plan for how you intend to walk the visitor through the property and all of the areas to which the tenant will have access. You should have an idea of which rooms and features are the most attractive and how you'll highlight them in the viewing process. For example, if one of the nicest areas of the accommodation is perhaps a balcony or a patio, show this space last and invite the tenant to sit and enjoy the space whilst you discuss cost and expectations. Each room in the accommodation will have its key selling features, so include in your viewing plan a way for you to highlight these as well. Traditionally, big selling points include features like:

- Large and open rooms
- Open-floor concepts
- Updated appliances and safety features
- Beautiful views
- Natural lighting
- Rooftop access, courtyards, gardens
- Walk-in wardrobes
- Ample and secured storage areas
- Central heating

Pre-Screening Questions to Ask Prospective Tenants

While you're showing the space, you can and should ask your own set of questions that will gain your insight into the prospect and help you pre-screen them. Start with some general questions that are not so invasive, such as:

- Where are you from?
- Do you come from a large family?
- What do you do for fun?
- What do you do for work?

Then you can start to ease into the more revealing and insightful questions as they pertain to subletting.

- Why are you moving?
- When do you plan to move?
- Are you living in a similar situation now?
- What's the earliest you can move in?
- What's your average monthly income? (The monthly income should be at least double the rent, roughly.)
- Will anyone be moving with you?
- Do you have pets?
- Do you smoke?
- Will you consent to a credit and background check?
- Will you be able to provide references?

From tenant to tenant, be sure to ask the same questions to all. This keeps everything fair and cannot be misconstrued as discrimination. There are other tricks to pre-screening as well, and though they don't involve asking questions, they can be very revealing. Keep a lookout for the following:

The applicant's opinion of the property - If the prospective tenant is overly enthusiastic, it can be a sign that they are lying about their impressions or that they are trying to overcompensate because they know they may have a tarnished rental background. If the individual is overly critical of the property, it may be a sign of a troublesome tenant or an attempt to negotiate a much lower cost of rent.

The applicant's general behaviour - Take note of whether the individual is polite to you and any current tenants that may be present. Similarly, note whether the applicant is respectful of the property; wiping their feet upon entry, closing doors quietly, or whether they make unusual requests. This again can be a sign of a troublesome tenant.

The applicant's appearance and vehicle - If a prospective tenant shows up to a viewing in dirty and dishevelled clothing, and their vehicle looks much the same, this can be a sign that the individual does not take care of themselves and their own property. This is an insight that they may not take care of your property either.

The applicant's preparedness and attentiveness - If a prospective tenant shows up to a viewing unprepared and has no questions, it leaves a lot of room for misunderstandings to grow. An interested tenant will come prepared and will ask relevant questions.

As the viewing process winds down with your prospective tenant, be clear about the next steps. It is at this point that you should communicate whether there is an application fee and ask them to submit an application.

Let the prospective tenant know that as part of the application process, you will be conducting a credit and background check and contacting references. Tenants can negotiate costs and other terms of your agreement, but do not feel as though you have to bend to these. It's much cleaner to require the same from every tenant that applies for the space. It's more than okay to explain to the prospect that these are the steps your business has put in place for the benefit and safety of all parties involved. Further, you can explain that by following these steps you're ensuring that each applicant is treated fairly and equally, and this is a requirement of the law. Allowing one applicant to skip the background check, for example, can be seen as a sign of discrimination, for which your business can be fined and penalised.

As a professional subletter, remember to not make any tenancy decisions on the spot, especially without having conducted the background check. Instead, let the applicant know you'll be conducting the checks over the course of the next day or so and that you'll be back in touch to let them know how it

goes and whether you'd like to proceed with
them. A phone call or email will be appropriate.
Let applicants know how to contact you should
more questions arise over the next few days.

Chapter 6:

Scaling for Success

You've made it to the last step in your successful path to profitable subletting and property management; preparing for greatness and growth in the coming business quarters and years to come. Though it may be a bit early for you to take action on any of these aspects of your business just yet, you should have them in mind and build them into your process. So take out that 12-month business plan and let's see where you can add in these ideas and goals.

Expanding Your Property Structure

Up until this point, you've likely been focused on the subletting model because of its ability to make you a fast profit and get your business officially in the door to the industry. As you begin to make a healthy profit and your costs have largely been repaid or dissolved, it's time to think about expanding that which you do. With the profit you make, surely a portion will be put back into the business and this includes more properties. At this point as yourself whether a buy-to-rent unit is within your reach and how it can fit into your plan. With a year of experience behind you, you've developed a solid understanding of what it takes to rent and manage tenants. Now how about making a greater profit in leasing out a unit you've purchased? You essentially become the property owner of a new unit and with all your expertise, can skip the middleman and rent directly to tenants.

A move like this can be risky so it will require a healthy dose of due diligence. If you purchase a place and mortgage it, are you still able to make a healthy profit after expenses? Owning your own property to rent out gives you the benefit of capital growth. The unit will, in theory, grow in value in the coming years and this means a growth in profit via renting or even selling in the future.

Similarly, many who start out with rent-to-rent

schemes transition into other real estate ventures such as fix-and-flip properties. In this scenario, you would purchase a property that falls well below the average cost of a new home. These are often properties that have been repossessed for non-payment or failure to adhere to the terms and conditions of a mortgage lender. In these cases, the property will need fixing. Perhaps this will be some interior remodelling or a new roof. Whatever needs to be done, the idea is to get in and do it quickly so that you can reposition the home back on the market. A fix-and-flip investment will obviously cost a fair chunk of money up front to make the repairs, but the profit made selling a home can well exceed what you're making through subletting.

That's not to say you cannot stick with the sublet models and be just as successful. If you've started with an AST sublet, consider adding an HMO or an accommodation model to your portfolio. If you've had success with one sublet model and you want to stick with it, that works, too. Consider your expansion in terms of acquiring more properties to manage. There's really not a wrong way to grow and expand, except for not growing and expanding. Pulling in profit is great, but your business needs direction, and it is through this direction and strategy that even greater profits await you.

Acquire a Team

Another way to grow and expand is to consider
adding employees to your payroll. If this is part of
your plan, remember that your business structure
must be such that you are no longer a sole trader,
but making this small business structure change can
mean more money faster. When you have a team
that you can delegate to, the process goes much
faster and you can acquire more properties and
tenants at a greater rate. For all the work you'll do
yourself over the course of a year, imagine if you
could pass the more time-consuming tasks to
others. Imagine if you could pay someone else to
run your marketing, conduct your viewings, run
background checks, and draw up the paperwork?
This will leave you open for the heavier business
decisions, and the development of your business'
next steps. Like the expansion into buy-to-rent or
fix-and-flip properties, hiring a team, even a small
one, is another upfront business cost you'll incur.

There are business structure costs to handle, such as
registering your business, ensuring it for employees,
offering at least minimum wage (but probably more
for the type of work being done), and offering
benefits. If this doesn't seem like a realistic step for
your next 12-month business plan, you can start
small. Consider continuing your business structure
as it is, but hiring a virtual assistant or a freelance

assistant to help you with some of your work. This individual can be paid a lower wage while still taking a good deal of time-consuming research and paperwork off of your own plate.

Grow the Marketing Game

At this point, there is perhaps no easier and quicker way to expand than to up your marketing game and keep it fresh. Even if this is the only strategy you act on in your next step to expansion, it is arguably the most important one. In your first year of business, you've been heavy with all of the responsibilities that come with a start-up. Now that these responsibilities have been achieved, you'll find yourself with more bandwidth in year two. Use this time to gain growth through marketing.

Get Intimate with Your Audience

After the time you've spent in the last year getting to know your audience, you've come away with better insights. For your property owners and for your tenants, it's time to refine. You can do this by analysing the top 20% of your customers. Profile them. Who is it that makes up the top 20% of your property owners, and likewise your tenants? Find the similarities amongst these audience members; location, financial aspects, humanistic qualities, wants and goals. By analysing, you'll be able to better pinpoint what makes up your best audience and what makes up the other 80%. It's now your goal to target the individuals that make up that top 20%. Advertise in places they will see. Offer value they seek. Set higher costs that they can still afford.

By doing so, you'll be attracting more of the people you want to work with, and less of the people you don't.

Utilise Local Directories

With just a bit of research, you can identify dozens of local directories in which to list your business. Don't limit this to only print; online local directories are just as, if not more, important. But don't neglect print directories, either. Take a look around the communities in which you work and pick up print directories where you can. Listing in these directories is free or possible with a nominal annual fee. Consider listing on directories like:

- Google My Business
- LandlordZone
- CitizensAdvice
- Bing Places
- 118Information
- ThePhoneBook
- Yelp
- FreeIndex
- MyLocalServices
- TouchLocal
- Scoot
- Yell.com
- HotFrog
- Brownbook

Gather Testimonials

You've had ample time to build a rapport with numerous property owners and tenants. Now, ask them for a testimonial. If you want to sweeten the deal, perhaps offer a small monetary compensation, such as a portion discount on rent for the month, or a gift certificate for a local dinner or movie. Ask these individuals to provide a written testimonial to either be given to you for use as you see fit, or online in any of the relevant directories that offer ratings and endorsements. If you have a business website or a social media page, add these testimonials for better exposure to a focused audience.

Website Improvements

Take the time to tune up your website, landing page, or social media accounts. Keep them fresh and relevant and refine the locations you target. Business websites often have opt-in marketing that allows visitors of the site to sign up for newsletters, blogs, and valuable downloadable content. Consider adding or improving these opt-in options and repositioning them on the page for greater visibility and engagement. Sidebars, headers, footers, and banners at the top or bottom of a specific piece of content can work very well. Give them a chance where they are (90 days for example) and then experiment with relocating them. If it's possible, hire a freelance digital marketing pro for their expertise in this area. Often, not only will you gain their expertise, but they often will carry out these steps for you, included in their cost.

Add a Call-to-Action

In addition to opt-in options, a business website, landing page, or social media page often includes at least one call-to-action (CTA). A call to action is an enticing offer that pulls interested parties into your sales circle. For example, you might offer an online tenant application that reduces or eliminates the application fee. This offer can pull in prospective tenants so you have less work to do in the hunt for them.

Radio Advertisement

Radio is not dead. In fact, running your ad or securing a small slot of time to talk with local radio jockeys, on-air can greatly increase your exposure. Despite assumptions, radio advertisements such as this can be more cost-effective than print ads, and it will reach a wider audience. This may not target your refined 20%, but you never know who's listening; a friend or contact of the top 20% could be listening and will happily pass along your information and your offer.

SEO and PPC Strategies

SEO, or Search Engine Optimisation can move you upwards on Google when individuals, both landlords and tenants, search for the services you offer. SEO practices increase the amount of traffic to your site and the quality of those visitors, simply by implementing keywords. The content you display on your site can be optimised to include the words that your audience is searching for so that when these individuals turn to Google for search help, they organically find your site. PPC, or pay-per-click is much like SEO, but monetised. Utilising keywords, advertisers can basically pay for visitors to click on their ads based on the keywords for which the visitor has searched. The ad then directs the visitor to the advertiser's website or landing page for more information, and ultimately, to follow the call to action.

Social Media Marketing Strategy

More and more often, we see local ads placed on Facebook and similar social media platforms. These ads work much the same way as a PPC campaign, but in a location (social media) that your audience is already using. These campaigns are easy to set for your top 20% audience target, as well. Facebook makes it relatively easy to set up these campaigns yourself, and you can run them for as little as £10 per day. Campaigns are generally set for as little as

30 days and during that time, Facebook presents your ad in the feeds of the audience for which you've set your targets. Again, you can do this yourself, or consider hiring a freelance social media manager to set this for you.

Get Involved the Community

When you position yourself in the communities in which you work, not only are you demonstrating your desire and ability to help the local communities, but you're cultivating free (or nearly free) advertisement for your business. Community involvement is an excellent method for building rapport.

Establish Yourself as an Authority

Take time to write a blog or a feature article in a local print. This opportunity can easily establish you as an experienced professional and authority in the industry. If you don't have the time to keep up with a blog, and you don't have the opportunity to write a feature article, consider hosting an online AMA (ask me anything) and inviting interested members of your target audience to participate. Visit sites like Business.com and Quora to find questions that pertain to your industry and answer these questions concisely and professionally. There are plenty of places to assert your authority and professionalism if you just look for them.

Volunteer or Sponsor

Search the communities you currently target or want to target and find local events that your business can volunteer to be a part of. These events don't need to necessarily be related to your business or industry, in fact, it can work better for you if they are not. If your business is not able to physically participate, sponsor someone locally who can. This can be as easy as agreeing to sponsor someone for a local 5k, craft fair, or cook-off that ultimately benefits the community. By doing this, you expose yourself to a greater portion of the community, and though this may not be your target market, much like the radio, your involvement will get your business noticed and your contact passed along to those in the community that are your target audience.

Contests and Promotions

Beyond getting involved in local events, you can create contests and promotions yourself. It makes sense if these are more directly related to your business. For example, if you're able to build rapport with a local cleaning service or furniture store, you may be able to strike a deal with them to promote their business alongside your own to offer a free cleaning service or furnishings to individuals moving to the area. Combine this with your radio advertising and you've got a successful, simple marketing strategy that's sure to reach a large number of people interested in the contest or promotion.

Advance Yourself

Do not get stagnant and stop learning. There are always new practices, new techniques, and updated regulations in the world of rent-to-rent. There will always be new and changing information you must keep up with in order to stay fresh and relevant and to position yourself and the professional and authority you want to be in your local area(s). You've already learned so much, but it's nothing compared to what you have yet to learn from other professionals, who much like I, can train you to avoid mistakes and capitalise on opportunities.

Training Courses

When the time comes to develop your acumen even further than you have already with the contents of this book, you will find an abundance of resources from which to learn. Online, you can find several courses or webinars pertinent to your study of rent-to-rent and related business. You should, by all means, research the hosts and lecturers of these courses to make sure you're learning from the best, instead of passing your hard-earned profit to a fly-by-night individual trying to make quick cash. Research the course material before you pay for it, to make sure you're not just rehashing information you've already learned and practiced.

Find out what the expectations are for you by the end of the course and if it involves any sort of certification or significant accomplishment by the end of the course. Many courses can be taken online, and many of those can be taken at your own pace. One small issue to watch out for in that case, is that sometimes when there is no time limit or accountability, it can be tempting to start the course but never finish it. If this sounds like something you might be guilty of, select a course that requires attendance at a certain time (usually via a webinar or live video call) and your completion of the course materials by a certain deadline.

In addition to online courses, live courses in your local area are often available multiple times a year. These are typically seminars that last one day or several days and by the completion of the course, you're guaranteed some form of certification and supplemental benefits. Not only will an option like this educate you, but it also provides an exclusive networking circle of other local professionals with whom to build a rapport. Courses and seminars that are live and in person can sometimes require the course director to present a higher level of authority and expertise, so though the course may cost a bit more than that of an online course, you may receive a much higher quality of valuable and useful information.

Coaches and Mentors

Courses are great, but the material is designed to
meet the needs of everyone. Courses don't do such
a good job at analysing your specific circumstances
and designed solutions that you specifically
need. To get help on a more personal level, seek
out a coach or mentor that will work with you
directly, on your own 12-month business plan, for a
longer period of time; sometimes throughout the
entire year and beyond. Indeed, a coach or mentor
will likely only support you for a fee, but this is well
worth the cost to be able to have an experienced and
dedicated professional in your corner.

Your coach or mentor will help you to develop
business strategies that will fit your exact goals and
budget. This individual will meet with you regularly
to build your identity, sharpen your marketing
approach, spot strengths, weaknesses, and dangerous
gaps in your process.   These professionals provide
accountability for your progress on these action
plans. With your own coach or mentor, you'll build
confidence more quickly, and receive the
encouragement and tough love needed to succeed.

Property Investment Secrets – Rent to Rent: You've Got Questions, I've Got Answers!

If you've enjoyed this book and you've learned as much from me as I hope you have, one of the best professional advancements you can make is to continue this course of education. The insight and tools I've offered you here do not stop here. You've made it through a wealth of information to begin your business, but now you can take it to the next level in the next book that supplements this one.

In the next book, you'll take what you've learned and distil it. You'll dive deeper into building your next business plan, your next marketing strategy, and your polished online and professional image. As you've read through this book, you've likely come up with some additional questions for each scenario. For example, what does it take to delegate work to a virtual assistant? What kind of work can you delegate? What kind of work is too specific to delegate? You might wonder how to go about devising a sales funnel opportunity on your own business website, and how to build a social media campaign that works effectively and quickly. You might be eager to find out more about what kinds of safety and security codes you'll need to adhere to in order to run the tightest ship possible.

The supplemental book will walk you through these challenges and much more. When you've been back and forth through the pages of this book; when you've practised and refined the processes herein; when you remember the words you've read by heart, new knowledge is waiting for you to grasp it and run with it. For all you've put in, there's still more to get out. Consider advancing to the next book, and accelerating your new profession.

Conclusion

Congratulations! You've completed Property Investment Secrets - Rent to Rent: A Complete Property Investing Guide! I hope this journey has been an exciting and informative one and I thank you for travelling with me as your guide. As you've walked with me, you've gathered a true sense of what a rent-to-rent business looks like and how it operates legally, professionally, and ethically. This already puts you out ahead of the pack.

What's more, you've learned the importance of developing a 12-month business strategy and how to use this document regularly as you search for properties, negotiate with property owners, and sublet the units you manage. You're now familiar with the process of establishing and registering your business and the small but significant steps in that process which you cannot skip or else you leave yourself and your business open and unprotected from liability, fines, and even criminal prosecution. This puts you miles ahead of most individuals out there on their various paths, trying to eke out a fast and furious profit through subletting.

You now have in your tool kit a 5-step process for finding viable properties. Along with this process, you have a comprehensive breakdown of the means for negotiating with property owners and how to close those deals. You're prepared to walk into a viewing of the unit with all the questions and concerns that may arise, plus how to begin and complete the application process for tenants.

At the end of your first 12-month period, you exactly which aspects of your business to focus on for annual growth in the coming 12-month period and how to select the strategies that will work best for you. You understand that this is just the beginning and you have much to still learn from others and experience yourself, but the path to that excellence is clear. This puts you lightyears ahead of the rest.

From this point on, you can walk into the world of rent-to-rent with confidence and knowledge that many never gain and actually lose sight of as they try to keep from sinking in a business they did not prepare for. But not you. You're far-removed from this floundering and deep in the lead; staring at success; staring at a healthy profit and prosperity; staring right in the eyes of an expanding business set for greatness on the horizon.

Take what you've learned here and implement it without hesitation. Find the pieces you now know you need and lock them into place. Set out with one deliberate foot in front of the other on the heels of your next victory. Return to these lessons often and as you go, augment them to serve you best.

It's true that a successful sublet business can be yours. The dream of working for yourself and gaining greater control and fortune through this business model is real. It's within your grasp. Now reach out and take it.

Printed in Great Britain
by Amazon

21573895R00109